D1114318

Lighthouses & Range Lights of Door County, Wisconsin

by

Peter Bosman

with illustrations
by Katie Bosman & Peter Bosman

Wm Caxton Ltd
Ellison Bay, Wisconsin
2000

Published by:

Wm Caxton Ltd
12037 Highway 42, Box 220
Ellison Bay, WI 54210

(920) 854-2955

Printed in the United States of America.

10   9   8   7   6   5   4   3   2   1

Library of Congress Cataloging-in-Publication Data

Bosman, Peter, 1948–
  Lighthouses & range lights of Door County, Wisconsin / by Peter Bosman with
illustrations by Katie Bosman & Peter Bosman.
    p. cm.
  Includes bibliographical references.
  ISBN 0-940473-38-0 (pbk. : alk.paper)
  1. Lighthouses--Wisconsin--Door County. 2. Door County (Wis.)--History. I. Title.

VK1024.W6B67 2000
387.1'55'0977563--dc21

                                                                                    00-022688

ISBN# 0-940473-38-0   Original paperback.

This book is set in a version of Palatino type chosen for its readability and attractiveness; it is printed on acid-neutral paper bound in sewn signatures and is intended to provide a very long useful life.

COVER PHOTO: The tug *Jimmy L.* shown passing the North Pierhead Light on the way into the Sturgeon Bay Ship Canal from Lake Michigan. Now owned and operated by Selvick Marine Towing Corporation of Sturgeon Bay, the *Jimmy L.* originally was a US Coast Guard vessel named the *Naugatuck.* Photo courtesy of Wendell Wilke, marine photographer.

Acknowledgements

Thanks to June Larson of the Door County Maritime Museum and to Joel and Mary Ann Blahnik, caretakers of the Chambers Island Lighthouse, whose input and advice on the manuscript has been extremely helpful; to BMC Dale Dempsey, Officer in Charge, and Seaman Brenda M. Kolp-Remer of the US Coast Guard Aids to Navigation Team, Green Bay, WI for providing valuable technical information and answering many questions; to George Koller, whose ongoing help and advice helped bring this book into being and see it through to completion; to my daughter Katie, and to Tom McKenzie, whose artistic and journalistic talents have added greatly to this book; and to my wife Mary and my daughter Carrie for their inspiration, patience, and support.

Special thanks to Dr. Steven Karges, whose research has provided detailed information on many of the lighthouses of Door County; his forthcoming book on the keepers of Door County's lighthouses will be of particular interest to anyone interested in maritime history.

Finally, thanks to all the people — including writers, photographers, illustrators, and researchers of the publications listed in the references — whose appreciation of Door County's past has helped to build a base from which future historical research can proceed.

DOOR COUNTY LIGHTHOUSE MAP

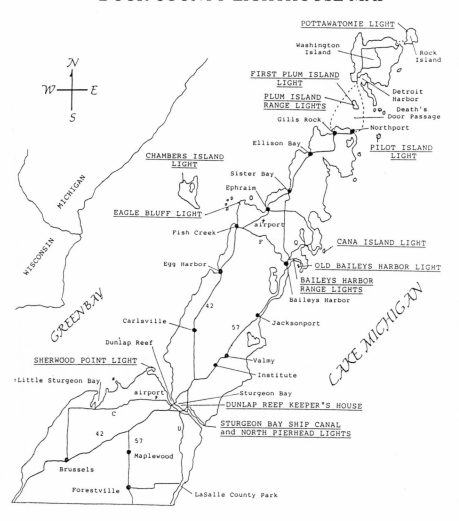

POTTAWATOMIE LIGHT

Washington
Island

Rock
Island

FIRST PLUM ISLAND
LIGHT

PLUM ISLAND
RANGE LIGHTS

Detroit
Harbor

Death's
Door Passage

Gills Rock

Northport

Ellison Bay

PILOT ISLAND
LIGHT

CHAMBERS ISLAND
LIGHT

Sister Bay

Ephraim

EAGLE BLUFF LIGHT

Fish Creek

airport

CANA ISLAND LIGHT

OLD BAILEYS HARBOR LIGHT

Egg Harbor

BAILEYS HARBOR
RANGE LIGHTS

Baileys Harbor

MICHIGAN

WISCONSIN

GREEN BAY

LAKE MICHIGAN

42

Carlsville

57

Jacksonport

Dunlap Reef

SHERWOOD POINT LIGHT

Valmy

Institute

Little Sturgeon Bay

airport

Sturgeon Bay

DUNLAP REEF KEEPER'S HOUSE

STURGEON BAY SHIP CANAL
and NORTH PIERHEAD LIGHTS

C

U

42

57

Maplewood

Brussels

Forestville

LaSalle County Park

Contents

Introduction

For many of us, lighthouses hold a great fascination, perhaps because they represent a tangible link to an earlier, simpler, and more romantic time, when graceful schooners sailed the Great Lakes.

In the early 1800s, however, the young American government had few romantic notions. During the preceding 200 years, the lands that were to become Door County had passed from the hands of Native Americans to the French, then to the British, and finally to the United States. The completion of the Erie Canal in 1825 opened an easy route to the entire Great Lakes region, and the problem of making the Great Lakes safe for ship navigation suddenly became very important, not only for defense of the territory, but also for commercial development. The federal government realized that there was a pressing need for lighthouses on the Great Lakes, and they shortly began to commission and build them.

The Door Peninsula's wealth of timber and stone resources led to its earliest development, and its configuration as a peninsula surrounded by water and 250 miles of shoreline meant that ships were the easiest and most natural way for resources, products, and people to come and go from the area. To accommodate this maritime trade, lighthouses were built. By 1900 Door County had more lighthouses than any other county in the United States.

In their relatively brief lives, the lighthouses and range lights of Door County have witnessed all phases of the evolution of commercial shipping on the Great Lakes. Wooden sailing vessels as well as steam-powered "lumber hookers" and passenger ships have plied county waters. Great steel cargo ships have been built in Door County and such vessels now carry iron ore past our shores.

As supply and demand for both lumber and stone dwindled, and as better roads were developed, fewer commercial ships came to Door County, making the lighthouses somewhat less important than before. Also, the peninsula's lighthouses became less important as navigational aids as modern radar and satellite navigation developed. However, they remain as valuable guides to many vessels, especially sport boaters and recreational sailors.

Door County's lighthouses and range lights are rich in history and have helped thousands of mariners to safe harbor, but today these beacons serve mainly as another kind of guide — to our past and to ourselves.

A Brief History of Lighthouses

An artist's conception of Pharos, the world's first recorded lighthouse, built about 280 BC at Alexandria, Egypt. No actual pictures of the lighthouse exist; the drawing is based on a description of a square base, an octagonal mid-section, and a round tapered tower atop which a large fire was kept burning. Pharos was considered one of the Seven Wonders of the Ancient World.

Some Famous Lighthouses in World History

The lighthouses of Door County are part of a long and rich tradition of helping to guide mariners and their ships safely to harbor, especially harbors with treacherous shoals, rocky shores, unpredictable winds, and fast-flowing currents.

Early Greek and Egyptian literature refers to fires kept burning at specific mountain locations. These wood fires provided smoke that could be seen by day and light that might be seen by night. They often were tended by teams from local villages who were in the service of merchants or governments with an interest in the safe arrival of sailing vessels.

In about 280 BC the first recorded lighthouse structure was completed on Pharos Island at the entrance to the harbor of Alexandria, Egypt. Pharos was one of the Seven Wonders of the ancient world. It is said to have been over 400 feet tall, with a huge fire kept burning on a platform at its top to guide ships. The lighthouse may have stood until the 13th century when it was finally toppled by an earthquake.

The Roman Empire also maintained lighthouses to mark the waterways of its far-flung Mediterranean lands. By AD 400, there were as many as thirty of these lights. Some of the more notable of them included towers at Ostia, near Rome, built about AD 50; a light at Boulogne, France built about AD 40; a light built at La Coruna, in Spain; and one built at Dover in Britain. These early lighthouses were monumental structures in terms of size, engineering, and construction; most were more than a hundred feet tall. At first, they were lit by wood fires on platforms at their top, but after the first century AD, some used candles or oil lamps with glass panes protecting the flame from the weather. The construction of these towers was very sound, and most of them outlasted the Roman Empire itself by many centuries. In addition to their function guiding ancient mariners, many of the early lighthouses also served as fortresses and lookout towers to defend against advancing enemies of the Roman Empire.

The period of European history from late in the 5th century through the 10th century is known as the Dark Ages. As the Roman Empire crumbled, the entire region was in a state of turmoil and economic stagnation. There was little maritime commerce during this period, and no lighthouses are known to have been built during this time span.

Newly organized nations began to emerge from the Dark Ages by 1100, and maritime trade began to revive around the Mediterranean and along other coasts of Europe. As this happened, many surviving light towers were restored and new lighthouses began to be built. The Italians built both the Lanterna of Genoa and a lighthouse at Meloria by the middle of the 12th century. The Emperor Charlemagne had the Boulogne tower rebuilt in 800; it remained in use until it collapsed in 1644.

During the 13th century the Hanseatic League, an organization of merchants in what is now northern Germany, was formed. It soon spread to surrounding towns, and eventually comprised a very widespread trading network in northern Europe. The League stimulated maritime commercial trade, and under its influence at least fifteen lighthouses were constructed along German and Scandinavian coasts by 1600. But the expansion of trade during this era outpaced the construction of lighthouses, and lights placed in church and castle towers along the coasts often served as navigational aids as well.

By the 16th century, Britain was becoming a powerful force in Europe, with a strong emphasis on maritime trade and sea power that eventually expanded into the far-reaching British Empire. The late 1600s see the beginning of the era of modern lighthouse construction, with the building of the first of the famous lighthouses on the Eddystone Rocks near Plymouth, England.

The Eddystone Light is a famous "modern" lighthouse, first built in 1698 on the Eddystone rocks off Plymouth, England. The view shown was redrawn from a drawing in the Library of Congress collection.

The first Eddystone Light was completed in 1698. Since that time, it has been rebuilt three times, and there is a rich history of personal triumphs, engineering innovations, and tragedies involved in the story of those lights. The fourth one is still standing, perched on the hazardous rocks outside Plymouth harbor, from which many ships began their journeys to the New World.

Boston Light was America's first lighthouse. It was built in 1716. Drawn from a US Coast Guard photograph of an early drawing.

The American Lighthouse Story

As the Dark Ages came to a close in Europe, explorers from that part of the world set out upon the ocean in hopes of finding new trade partners and trade routes. They especially sought a water route to the Far East, and in 1492, Columbus sailed west from Spain to try to find one. As every schoolchild knows, he found instead the islands of the West Indies, and he returned to Spain with tales of a vast and rich New World. These tales kindled the imaginations of many others, who set out to make their fortunes and establish a new life, away from the confines and strictures of Europe. Initially, most came for plunder and conquest, but, by the late 1500s, settlements by transplanted communities were attempted.

The earliest colonies failed, but settlers continued to come, and eventually some survived. The New England area saw many attempts, and, by the late 1600s, several of the settlements there had established themselves permanently and the development of America had begun.

Though the early colonists tried to be self-sufficient, they were not able to provide for all their own needs, and they continued to depend on trade to supply goods that they could not produce themselves. So, as settlements developed, the need for trade also increased. Even between colonies, ships were the most practical and economical method of transporting people and goods, and as America grew, the main trade centers were in areas that could be reached by ship. As more and more ships plied the New England coast, navigation hazards there led local merchants to petition for America's first lighthouse — the Boston Light — built in 1716.

The building of lighthouses in America closely reflects our nation's economic development. As a coastal area was settled, lighthouses were built to make navigation and trade there easier and safer, and as demand for new products or raw materials grew, lighthouses were built to improve the navigation and transportation related to them. Thus, lighthouses spread down the Atlantic Coast from 1716 through 1875, along the Gulf Coast from 1825 to 1872, through the Great Lakes from 1818 to 1910, and up and down the West Coast from 1854 to 1926, as each of those regions developed economically.

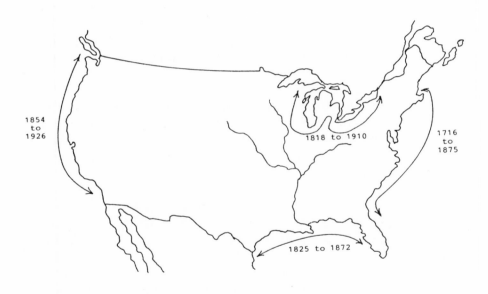

The building of America's lighthouses paralleled our nation's development. The time periods indicated on this map show when the lighthouses were built. Lighted navigational aids were also built along the length of the Mississippi River and its tributaries which was, and still is, a major water route providing commercial access to America's mid-section.

Lighthouses Come
to the Great Lakes

The First People

Before the first lighthouse was built on the Great Lakes, signaling the beginning of modern development and commerce, the region had already passed through a long transitional period.

Native American peoples were the first people to inhabit the wild and pristine Great Lakes basin, which had been carved out by the glaciers of the Ice Age. They moved into the region as the glaciers receded, beginning some 10,000 years ago, and they were well established across the entire region long before Europeans first arrived from across the Atlantic.

Northern European mariners reached Iceland, Greenland, and the Atlantic coast of Canada (including Newfoundland) some-time after AD 1000, but there is no convincing evidence that they reached the Great Lakes of North America. Samuel de Champlain apparently was the first European to reach the Great Lakes region. He and his companions made it to Georgian Bay and Lake Huron in 1615, and other French explorers soon followed. Jean Nicolet led a party traveling by canoe along the northern shores of Lake Huron and Lake Michigan in 1634. They crossed the waters to Rock Island and discovered the Door Peninsula. In 1667, Nicolas Perrot began to trade for furs on Green Bay, traveling by canoe, and in 1673 Father Jacques Marquette and Louis Jolliet proceeded up the Fox River from Green Bay on a trip across Wisconsin that nearly reached the Mississippi River.

In 1679 Robert Cavalier Sieur de LaSalle became the first person to venture through the Great Lakes in a commercial sailing vessel, a harbinger of the changes to come. The story of his landing in Door County and of the mysterious fate of his now-legendary ship the *Griffin* have earned a special place in the history of Door County and of the Great Lakes.

The Legend of the *Griffin*

LaSalle's ship *Griffin* was a sailing vessel of approximately sixty-five feet, equipped with cabins for the crew, cannons for defense, and a cargo space equivalent to that of seventy-five to a hundred fur-laden canoes. Much of what is known of LaSalle's voyage comes from the writings of a missionary named Father Louis Hennepin who accompanied LaSalle in hopes of converting the natives to Christianity.

In August of 1679, LaSalle and his crew departed in the newly completed *Griffin* from the site where it was built at the mouth of Cayuga Creek, about five miles upriver from Niagara Falls, between Lake Ontario and Lake Erie. They were bound for Lake Michigan. LaSalle's goal was to earn a large profit in the fur trade, with which he meant to fund further explorations into the interior of the New World.

La Salle's crew was made up of seasoned ocean sailors, but they were very surprised at the fury of storms on the Great Lakes. A great storm was in progress when the *Griffin* reached the islands off the tip of the Door Peninsula. With the help of a Native American (probably Chief Onanguisse of the Potawatomi), who paddled out onto the rough lake to meet them, La Salle and his crew made safe anchorage, most probably at Detroit Harbor on Washington Island.

The Chief impressed upon the travelers that even though their ship had survived the storm, it was unlikely that they could make it out of the vicinity before winter's arrival. LaSalle

10

recognized the Chief's wisdom and "resolved to send back his barque from this place, and to continue his route by canoe," according to Hennepin.

Robert LaSalle's legendary ship *Griffin* was the first recorded sailing vessel on the waters of the Great Lakes. After taking on its first cargo of furs in September of 1679, probably at Detroit Harbor on Washington Island, the ship disappeared on the return trip to Niagara Falls. The fate of the *Griffin* remains a matter of speculation and mystery to this day.

LaSalle had sent men well in advance of his trip to begin trading for furs, and enough had been gathered to make the trip profitable. The furs were loaded aboard the *Griffin*, and the ship sailed on 18 September 1679, manned by five sailors and a clerk and headed back to Niagara Falls.

LaSalle and his fourteen remaining men proceeded southward down the Lake Michigan shore in canoes. Plagued by foul cold weather, the group nearly perished of exposure and starvation before being rescued by Pottowatomis in southern Door County at what is now LaSalle County Park, ten miles south of Sturgeon Bay on County Hwy U (see map).

Meanwhile, the *Griffin* vanished. Her fate remains a mystery to this day. Hennepin later speculated that the ship probably had anchored due to bad weather "in the north of Lake Dauphin [Lake Michigan]" and then, against the advice of Native Americans who were there, had set sail again, only to meet disaster on the high seas of the Great Lakes. On the other hand, the fur trader Nicolas Perrot reported that members of the Ottawa tribe (with whom he traded) had found the *Griffin* at an anchorage on Lake Michigan's north shore, had murdered the crew in the night, and had burned the vessel. The Ottawas were hostile because of the threat the *Griffin* posed to their fur-trading and fur-transportation business, but there is no way to absolutely confirm Perrot's report.

In *The Fate of The Griffon* [sic], Harrison John Maclean provides evidence of having found the *Griffin* in Georgian Bay on Lake Huron. He points out that LaSalle had many enemies, even among his French countrymen, and he reports that Nicholas Perrot had tried to poison LaSalle while working for him, which could cast doubt on Perrot's version of the disappearance of the *Griffin*.

Over the years, many other people have claimed to have found wreckage of the *Griffin*, but none have ever been able to prove their claims beyond doubt. Thus the exact fate of the *Griffin* remains unknown, though people continue to search and wonder.

Battles for Great Lakes Territories

During the 1700s and early 1800s, several factors — notions of empire building by the French and British, a losing struggle to save their way of life by Native Americans, and the stirring of the American movement for independence — resulted in a long period that saw considerable conflict and danger but little development in the Great Lakes basin. During this period, several wars were waged — the French and Indian War, the American War of Independence, and the War of 1812 — until finally, after 1815, a lasting dominion over the Great Lakes was established by the new United States of America. The fate of the Native American way of life was sealed, and an era of rapid and largely uncontrolled development was set to begin.

The Floodgates to the Great Lakes are Opened

Even as battles of the American War of Independence still raged, colonists were turning their attention to westward expansion beyond the Appalachians. They established wagon routes across the mountains by 1800, though the journey was slow and arduous in their Conestoga wagons drawn by horses or by oxen.

Soon, however, ships were being built on the Great Lakes, and in 1818 a light tower was built at Fort Niagara, below Niagara Falls, where the Niagara River enters Lake Ontario. In 1819, the first lighthouse on the upper Great Lakes — the Presque Isle Light — was built on Lake Erie. It was obvious that development and expansion in the Great Lakes basin would be much easier and less expensive if a water route could be found from the Atlantic Ocean to the Great Lakes, but the barriers to a water connection were formidable — the Appalachians blocked most routes, and there was also the problem that the surface of Lake Erie is 570 feet higher than the Atlantic. At first the obstacles seemed insurmountable, but visionary engineers thought they might be able to construct a canal connecting the Hudson River with Lake Erie. In 1817, New York Governor DeWitt Clinton became convinced that the engineers' plan would work, and digging was begun.

The Erie Canal was completed across New York state in 1825, linking the Great Lakes to the Atlantic via the Hudson River. It was a staggering undertaking that involved digging 363 miles of channel, constructing eighty-three locks, and building eighteen viaducts. But, in one stroke, it overcame the barriers posed by mountains and lake elevation and literally opened the floodgates of westward expansion.

On a turnpike, four horses were required to move a ton-and-a-half wagon load of freight eighteen miles in a day; on the canal, the same four horses could draw a hundred-ton boat load twenty-four miles in a day.

Encouraged by the success of the Erie Canal, many other manmade waterways were planned and constructed throughout the Great Lakes region during the next 100 years. These man-made waterways created more numerous and more accessible shipping routes that heralded an explosion of development for the entire Great Lakes basin.

In 1800, the total population of the Old Northwest (the present states of Ohio, Michigan, Indiana, Illinois, and Wisconsin) was about 50,000. By 1820, this number had increased to about 800,000; by 1860, it stood at about 9 million, a third of the entire population of the United States at that time. Shipping was the main means of transport throughout the area; mostly, people and goods were moved west, while farm products, lumber, and coal were hauled east.

As new ports sprang up and shipping increased, the perils of Great Lakes navigation became more and more apparentto everyone. To attract commerce and provide safe passage to these lighthouses were needed, and they began to be commissioned throughout the Great Lakes. In 1832 the Chicago Harbor Light was completed; it was the first lighthouse on Lake Michigan.

The Erie Canal, completed in 1825, was an engineering and construction triumph. It provided a long practical 363-mile waterway linking the Great Lakes and the Atlantic Ocean, thus opening the gates to the development of the Great Lakes basin. From the writings of the author's great great grandmother, Susan Foxwell Moyle, "We landed in New York May 19, 1842. We spent no time in NY, but sought Wisconsin where our friends were. Our little band of emigrants went up the Hudson River and through the Erie Canal to the Great Lakes. After six weeks on the ocean, the men of the party were very glad to walk along the banks of the canal, getting acquainted with the animals and the vegetation of this their new homeland."

Door County Lighthouses — The Beginning of an Era

Door County was the first part of Wisconsin to be discovered by the early French voyageurs, but it fell back into relative obscurity for the next 150 years after that earliest contact. The first lighthouse to be built in Door County was the Pottawatomie Lighthouse on Rock Island in 1836. At that time the Door Peninsula and its islands were merely an obstacle on the route from Lake Michigan to Green Bay, rather than destinations in themselves, and the Pottawatomie Lighthouse stood at the end of the obstacle.

In 1836 Increase Claflin became the first European settler to move into Door County from the south, and in 1837 a small fishing village came to Rock Island, but it was not until 1848 that the Door Peninsula was truly rediscovered by the outside world. A man by the name of Captain Bailey was en route to Milwaukee from Buffalo with a load of immigrants when he was caught by an easterly gale that forced him to seek refuge in an uncharted bay which eventually became known as Baileys Harbor. There he found timber and building stone, and he took samples back to Milwaukee.

Bailey's discovery of a good harbor and of potentially profitable cargoes seems to have caused quite a stir in Milwaukee. The owner of Captain Bailey's ship, a man named Alanson Sweet, apparently had some political influence, and he soon persuaded the Wisconsin Legislature to organize the area as Door County. Sweet immediately began building a port from which he planned to export building stone, cordwood, and lumber to the rapidly growing cities of Milwaukee and Chicago, and he convinced the federal government of the need for a lighthouse. In 1851 the Baileys Harbor Lighthouse became the first lighthouse built to serve a port on the Door Peninsula. For unknown reasons, Sweet did not follow through with his business plans for Baileys Harbor. Other businessmen took his place, however, and the lumber industry was soon developing nicely, and the stone business to a lesser degree. As land in the area was cleared of timber, settlers (including some of the lumber workers) purchased tracts of land, and successful farms soon began to appear.

Shortly after Baileys Harbor was established, other villages began to spring up on the bays that punctuate Door County's 250 miles of shoreline. Soon these other settlements were exporting lumber, stone, fish, and ice to the cities further south, and, as more settlers arrived, more supplies and goods had to be imported. Since the roads were few and poor, virtually all of this trade moved by ship. The "golden" era of Door County lighthouses and shipping had begun. By the end of the century, Door County would have more lighthouses than any other county in the United States.

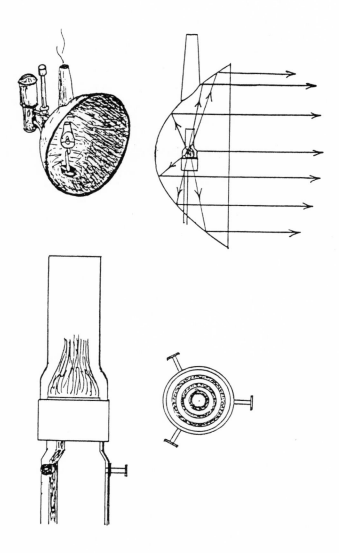

Hutchinson's parabolic reflector (top drawings) and Argand's oil lamp (bottom drawings) with its efficient, smokeless, concentric wicks were invented in the late 1700s. Combined, they produced a very bright light beam. They were used in the early days of many of Door County's early lighthouses.

The Lighthouses, Range Lights, & Their Keepers

The Lighthouses

The purpose of a lighthouse is to help ships to navigate safely in hazardous waters, particularly at night. Thus, the essence of a lighthouse is the light at its top.

The earliest lighthouses burned wood on open platforms for illumination. Later, candles and oil lamps were used. After about 1550, coal fires lit some lighthouses, and mariners preferred coal because it gave the brightest light. But a lighthouse might burn 300 tons of coal a year, a formidable problem for those who carried the coal to the top.

However, all these fuels produced large amounts of smoke which continually blackened the glass lantern panes that had been added to many lighthouses to protect the fires from the weather. Also, the intensity of these lights was quite low and their visible range was poor, especially in bad weather when they were needed most.

In 1777, William Hutchinson of Liverpool, England invented the parabolic reflector, made originally of glass mirrors and later of polished, silver-plated metal. The parabolic reflector focused the light into a bright narrow beam, greatly increasing the visible range of lighthouses.

Also, in 1782, a new type of virtually smokeless oil lamp was invented by Aime Argand, a Swiss scientist. It used a hollow wick which produced a very bright flame, and several of these wicks could be placed together into one lamp.

Combining Hutchinson's parabolic reflector with Argand's new lamp produced lighthouse beams that were hundreds of times brighter than any previous method of illumination. Several reflectors and lamps could be placed in a lighthouse to beam light in different directions, and, in 1781, the first system was invented to rotate the light apparatus so that the beam could be seen from any direction. The first Door County lighthouses used variations of the parabolic reflector/Argand oil lamp system, but light technology has changed a great deal since the Pottawatomie Lighthouse first projected its beacon using that system.

In 1822, a French physicist named Augustin Fresnel invented a new glass lens that used what is called a dioptric system. In Fresnel's system, a set of concentric glass prisms are arranged in a "beehive" shape, and light from the lamp is refracted into a powerful beam which is emitted from the middle part of the apparatus through a magnifying lens or lenses.

Fresnel lenses were produced in France and were made in several sizes or "orders" numbered from one to six. A "first order" Fresnel lens could be as much as six feet in diameter, twelve feet tall, and weigh several tons; while a "sixth order" Fresnel lens is about a foot in diameter and a foot and a half high. Fresnel lenses were a great improvement over parabolic reflectors and effectively doubled the range of the average lighthouse.

Due apparently to politics and cronyism, Fresnel lenses were not installed in American lighthouses until the 1850s. However, once the Lighthouse Board was established in 1852, Fresnel lenses were put into virtually all new and existing American lighthouses, including those in Door County, and many are still in use today. The largest Fresnel lenses installed in Door County lighthouses were "third order" lights, about three and a half feet in diameter and over four and a half feet tall. Both the Cana Island Lighthouse and the Sturgeon Bay Ship Canal Lighthouse still operate these magnificent "third order" Fresnel lenses.

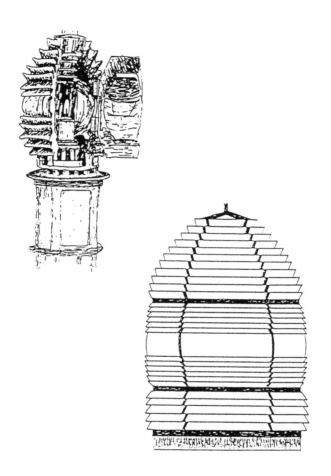

Following the inventions of the parabolic reflector and Argand oil lamp, the Fresnel lens, invented in 1822 by French physicist Augustin Fresnel, represented the next great improvement in lighthouse illumination, doubling the range of previous systems. The lenses illustrated above include a 4th Order lens, about 3 feet tall, in the top drawing, and a 3rd Order lens, about 4 1/2 feet tall, in the lower drawing. After the 1850s most US lighthouses, including those of Door County, used Fresnel lenses.

By the late 1850s, improved oil lamps had been developed, and, due to the near-extinction of the whales, lard oil had replaced sperm-whale oil in lighthouses throughout the US, including Door County. However, by 1885, kerosene burned in incandescent oil-vapor lamps had become the norm, and they continued to be used until they were replaced by electric lamps in the 1920s.

Today's lighthouse lamps are all electric, and many are being converted to run off solar-powered batteries. An automatic bulb changer now turns a new bulb on when one burns out and rotates it into position, and modern technology can now produce plastic lenses that are just as effective as the Fresnel lens, but much smaller, lighter, and less expensive.

Fog is a bane of navigation against which a lighthouse beacon may be completely ineffective. Thus, in addition to their lights, many lighthouses had fog signals to help mariners to find their way. Several different types of fog signals were in common use. Some consisted of a bell operated by a suspended weight system similar to that of a pendulum clock; others used a steam whistle operated by a steam boiler; still others employed a compressed air siren powered by an internal combustion engine. In recent times electric horns have replaced most other types of fog signals.

The Plum Island lighthouse, the Pilot Island lighthouse, and the Sturgeon Bay North Pierhead lighthouse all had steam-powered fog signals. Pilot Island and Sturgeon Bay North Pierhead each had two steam fog signals in their early days. One could serve as a backup signal in case of a malfunction, and also, both could be used together, alternating blasts, as it took considerable time to build up steam pressure.

When visibility is good, the distinctive shapes and colors of individual lighthouses allow ship captains to identify them visually and to use them to pinpoint an exact location. During the 1850s the Lighthouse Board developed a reliable "Light List" which was updated annually as an aid to ship captains. The list included the location and a physical description of each lighthouse, and it specified light colors and patterns as well as fog signal types and patterns that helped to identify them. The Light List is still available today and is updated annually by the U.S. Coast Guard.

Every lighthouse is designed and built to meet the specific needs of the site where it is located. Tower heights, light sizes, construction materials, keeper's dwellings, and fog signals, for example, could all be altered to make the most effective lighthouse for a given situation. This is reflected in the variety of design and architecture seen in Door County's lighthouses.

However, while each lighthouse must necessarily be unique due to the specific location where it is built, it is also apparent that lighthouses built in the 1800s (including all of those built in Door County) often are similar in design. Whenever possible, there was an attempt to standardize design and construction materials, and this made great economic sense in terms of design costs, materials procurement, and the efficiency of construction crews.

For example, the Chambers Island lighthouse and the Eagle Bluff lighthouse were both built in 1868, and they are very similar to one another. Also, the Sherwood Point lighthouse, built in 1883, is virtually identical to one built in 1884 on the other side of Lake Michigan at Harbor Point on Little Traverse Bay, and the Baileys Harbor Range Lights, built in 1869, also have a twin in the Presque Isle Range Lights built in 1870 on Lake Huron.

The original cost of Door County lighthouses varied, but most of them averaged about $12,000. Crews specializing in lighthouse construction (many of them from Detroit) were sent in to do the work, though local craftsmen sometimes were hired to assist. Most projects were begun in the spring; when things went well, a crew of twenty men could complete a lighthouse in about four months.

Construction materials were brought to the lighthouse sites by ship, and this was often the most hazardous part of the building process. Most sites were located in areas of dangerous waters exposed to wind and waves, with rocky shoals and shorelines. Many areas had imposing cliffs up which materials and supplies had to be hoisted.

The earliest Door County lighthouses were constructed of stone, but, as brick became commercially available, it became the preferred building material. Some wood construction was also used at sites where their was less harsh exposure to the weather. Light towers were either square, round, or octagonal and were attached to or built into the keeper's dwelling.

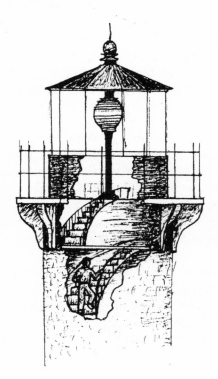

A cutaway view of a typical lighthouse tower construction.

Both the Sturgeon Bay Ship Canal lighthouse and the Plum Island Rear Range Light were built in the 1890s and reflect the then-new style of steel tower construction. The Cana Island lighthouse originally was a brick tower; however, in 1902, after decades of storms had caused the brickwork to deteriorate, it was encased in a steel shell. Each of these lighthouses has an enclosed watch room at the top of the tower, directly below the lantern room. From these watch rooms, keepers or life-saving crews were able to get a good sheltered view of the surrounding area. The watch rooms also contained some of the machinery for the large lenses and lamps in the lantern room just above.

All of Door County's lighthouses, except the Baileys Harbor Range Lights, have or had open platforms with railings at the base of the enclosed lantern room. These platforms could be used as lookout platforms when needed, and they also enabled keepers to do maintenance and clean the glass panes of the lantern room.

The Range Lights

Range lights are a specialized type of lighthouse structure which help to guide a ship on a specific course. They usually are built in areas where navigation is especially restricted and hazardous, such as in passages with many islands or shoals. They also frequently are used to mark narrow deep-water channels into a port, and also to mark river channels.

A set of range lights consists of two lights that define the line of a safe course into a harbor or through a set of barriers. The rear range light may be set a considerable distance behind the front range light and is also placed above the level of the front range light. Thus, when a ship is in a position such that the higher rear light lines up above the lower front light, the ship's crew knows that the ship is on the course marked by the range lights.

25

There were several sets of range lights in Door County: the Plum Island Range Lights are still in use; the Baileys Harbor Range Lights are no longer active, and the Dunlap Reef Lighthouse in Sturgeon Bay also was part of a set of range lights. The Sturgeon Bay Ship Canal Lighthouse and Ship Canal North Pierhead Light are not technically a set of range lights, though they often are used to serve that function by smaller ships; large commercial vessels follow a deep-water approach to Sturgeon Bay which is not on a direct line with the lights, but the relative positions of the lights can still be used as a reference point. Also, range lights help guide ships through the ship channel of Sturgeon Bay.

The Keepers

A lighthouse keeper's main job was to keep the lamp lit and bright from sundown to sunup during every night of the shipping season and to perform all the chores associated with maintaining the facility. This was a great responsibility, since mariners often staked their lives on the keepers' skills and dependability. There are many stories of heroic rescues from shipwrecks that have made lighthouse keepers legendary, but their true heroism lay in their relentless dedication to maintaining their lights under the most adverse conditions and in the most isolated places on the shores, islands, and reefs of the Great Lakes.

Lighthouse keepers and their families maintained their sometimes lonely but always vital vigils for more than a century. However, by the 1920s, electricity and twentieth-century automation had begun to replace the keepers. In 1939 the U.S. Coast Guard took over operation of the lighthouse system. Some of the previous keepers chose to stay on at their lighthouses, but Coast Guard personnel took over as keepers of the remaining non-automated lights. Electric timers were installed to turn lights on and off, burned out lights were automatically replaced, and the new high-powered sealed lenses did not need constant cleaning.

Sherwood Point lighthouse, near Sturgeon Bay, was the last manned American lighthouse on the Great Lakes. In 1983, exactly 100 years after it opened, the Sherwood Point lighthouse became fully automated and the era of live-in lighthouse keepers was over for this region.

Direction-finding radio beacons, radar, and satellite navigation systems have made lighthouses less vital to commercial vessels than they once were, but the lights still play an important role. They back up the high-tech navigation systems, and they are primary navigation aids on the thousands of smaller boats that don't have the advanced technology.

The New Keepers of the Lights

Even though the lighthouses are now automated and have modern equipment, the elements of nature remain as violent and harsh as ever, and constant work is needed to keep the lights functioning. Although lighthouses no longer have keepers on-site to keep them in working order, there is still a group of dedicated men and women who carry on the vigilant tradition of the former keepers. The Door County lights are kept lit by the U.S. Coast Guard Aids to Navigation Team based in Green Bay.

The members of the Aids to Navigation Team are responsible for maintenance and repairs on a total of ninety-four lighthouses, buoys, and other navigational aids distributed from Escanaba, MI to Manitowoc, WI, including all the Door County lights. They work in conjunction with the Coast Guard ship *Mobile Bay* based in Sturgeon Bay, which tends those buoys that are in deeper water and accessible by ship.

Automation and modern technology have simplified the maintenance of individual lighthouses and other navigation aids, but the sheer volume of sites maintained makes the task of the nine members of the Aids to Navigation Team no easier than the duties of former lighthouse keepers. The team does a yearly inspection and basic maintenance at each of the lighthouses and navigation aids. They then schedule return trips to sites as needed to upgrade or repair equipment, though they are also on call and go immediately to make repairs at any site that has a reported malfunction. The team has its own boat that allows them to reach all aids that are not accessible by land, and, when necessary, they call in the *Mobile Bay* or a Coast Guard helicopter to bring supplies or provide assistance.

One of the team's goals has been to standardize equipment as much as possible to make maintenance and repairs quicker, easier, and more cost effective. Unfortunately, the Aids to Navigation Team has neither the time nor the budget to fully maintain former keeper's dwellings or the grounds at some lighthouse sites. Pilot Island is an example of this. They maintain safe access for personnel to the light tower, and they keep the light in good working order, but parts of the keeper's dwelling and the surrounding grounds and buildings have fallen into disrepair.

Whenever possible, the Coast Guard works with other government agencies and with interested preservation groups to allow them to restore and maintain historically significant lighthouse sites.

The members of the Aids to Navigation Team that maintains the lights at Door County's lighthouses are really the modern-day lighthouse keepers, and they are just as dedicated as the men and women of the past in striving to keep the waters of Door County safe for ships and mariners.

The Lifesavers

During the past 150 years, the lighthouses of Door County have helped to guide thousands of ships and their crews safely through the waters of Lake Michigan and Green Bay. All too frequently, however, human effort and technology have been of no avail against the powerful storms, winds and waves on those waters, and hundreds of ships have been lost on the Great Lakes, sometimes due to natural forces, sometimes from human error or faulty equipment. Thus, to complement the preventive measures provided by the lighthouses, there long has also been a brave corps of lifesavers on Door County shores who stood always ready to wade in and help calamities occurred.

Lighthouse keepers often were members of this corps of lifesavers, along with many ordinary citizens. Also, the captains and crews of Great Lakes ships have been notoriously unselfish in risking their own lives to help fellow mariners. There are many stories of ship crews being rescued through heroic efforts of lifesavers.

The first lifesaving station in Door County was built at the Sturgeon Bay Ship Canal by the Federal Life-Saving Service in 1886, and, by 1896, there were stations at Baileys Harbor and on Plum Island. Two lifesaving stations are still active in Door County, both operated by the US Coast Guard — one on Washington Island (where the Plum Island station moved in 1991), the other at Sturgeon Bay.

In the early days, each station had a keeper as well as a crew of men known as surfmen who lived either at the station or nearby. The surfmen patrolled the shores at night and spent their days in watchtowers. Their hours were long and their working conditions were often miserable. When a shipwreck occurred, the surfmen had to haul their lifesaving equipment to the site of the wreck, either on beach carts weighing as much as a thousand pounds or in hand-powered surfboats. They often had to work at great distances from their stations and in the worst imaginable weather.

Today, life-saving equipment and techniques are much improved, and modern commercial vessels don't need help as often as older ships did. But, whether a ship in trouble is a large commercial vessel or a small pleasure boat, lifesavers today still sometimes must challenge the Great Lakes under the worst possible conditions in their efforts to help others in trouble.

Ships and Cargoes of Door County

During the 1800s, a unique and beautiful fleet of sailing schooners graced the waters of Door County and the Great Lakes. They were designed to carry maximum cargo and yet were able to enter shallow bays with their retractable centerboards. Their tall masts and thousands of square feet of sail allowed them to move very fast. Schooner rigging (with fore-and-aft-sails) made the ships easier to handle with a small crew than the square-rigged ships of the ocean, and better able to maneuver and to head up into the wind. One such vessel was the *Lake Forest*, a three-masted, 147-foot schooner built at Little Sturgeon in 1869. She once carried 500 tons of ice from near Escanaba in the upper peninsula of Michigan to Buffalo, New York, in only seventy-two hours, one of the fastest such voyages on record.

Today, such great schooners and their voyages are only memories, but the *Madeline*, a modern replica of an early schooner out of Traverse City, MI, helps to keep those memories alive by visiting ports on the Great Lakes as part of various maritime festivals and celebrations — including some in Door County. Another replica three-masted Great Lakes schooner, designed in Sturgeon Bay, is being constructed in Milwaukee. When completed, she too will sail the Great Lakes and help to take us back to those romantic schooner days.

Most of Door County's lighthouses were built during the schooner era. At that time, Door County's major exports were lumber for construction, cordwood for fuel, ice for keeping food cold, and stone for buildings, breakwaters, and other structures. These materials were shipped primarily to the rapidly developing cities of Chicago and Milwaukee and to the southern Lake Michigan area. On the return voyages, they carried people and supplies back to the newly settled and rapidly expanding communities of the Door peninsula. However, even before the schooner era had reached its peak, steam-powered ships were being developed, and the advantages of steam navigation ultimately destined the magnificent and romantic sailing ships to extinction as commercial vessels.

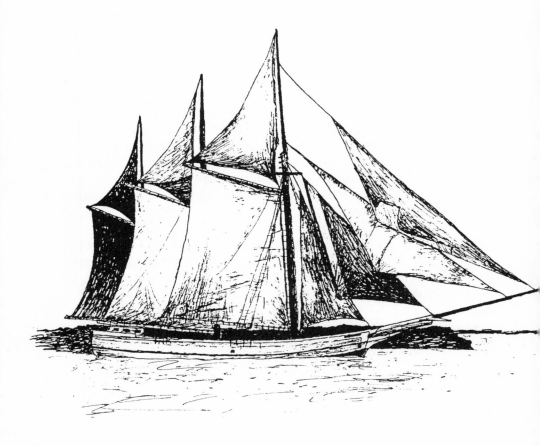

The schooner *Lake Forest*, built in Door County at Little Sturgeon in 1869. A typical example of the unique Great Lakes schooner design of the 1800s, this ship was known for her exceptional speed. Drawn from a photograph in *Schooner Days in Door County*.

In that era, most Door County communities were without railroads, and many lacked passable roads. Thus, they continued to rely on water transport for supplies and exports, and all sorts of ships — schooners, smaller sailing craft, and all sorts of steamships, including both sidewheelers and propeller-driven craft — plied Door County waters in ever-increasing numbers. By 1860, 369 steamships and 1207 sailing ships were registered on the Great Lakes.

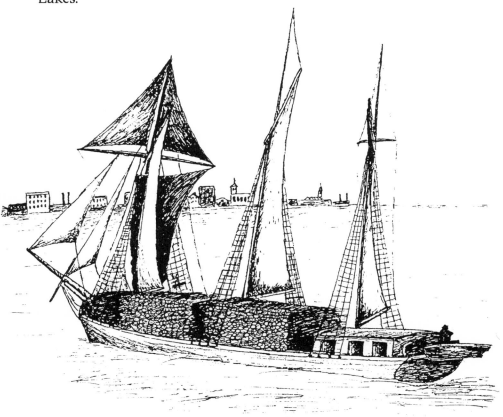

The schooner *Lucia A. Simpson*, built in 1875, delivering a load of lumber to a southern Lake Michigan port. She retired to Sturgeon Bay in 1929 after being damaged in a squall off Algoma, burned to the waterline in a fire in 1935, and some of her charred timber remains probably still lie under the docks of what is now Bay Shipbuilding Corporation.

At about this time a type of craft called a "lumber hooker" became common on the lakes. "Hookers" were named for similar craft from the Hook of Holland in Europe and were the forerunners of later Great Lakes freighters in that they had steam-driven propellers, forward-mounted wheelhouses, and crew quarters and engines in the rear, leaving the entire mid-section open to haul cargo. Hookers were built primarily of oak, long a favorite material for ship hull construction, and they became a common sight in Door County, carrying loads of lumber, stone and other materials.

However, as oak became more and more scarce, the new iron and steel technology was forging an industrial revolution in America which would change the entire nature of development in the Great Lakes area and have a large impact on Door County. The

The "lumber hooker" *Philetus Sawyer,* built in Green Bay and named after the US Senator who was influential in getting legislation passed which led to the completion of the Sturgeon Bay Ship Canal and the Ship Canal North Pierhead Light and breakwater.

lower Great Lakes area became a world center for steel production. The massive iron-ore deposits in the Mesabi Range northwest of Lake Superior began to provide the major cargo of the Lakes, and the ships that hauled that ore began increasingly to be constructed of iron and steel made from the ore they were hauling.

In the 1860s, two-thirds of the ship tonnage on the Great Lakes was still sail, and lumber and grain accounted for over two-thirds of the cargo. By 1882, the number of steamships matched the number of sailing vessels; by 1910, almost 90 percent of the actively operating ships were steam-powered, virtually all new ships were being built of steel, and over half the shipping tonnage was iron ore. Lumber and grain shipments had dropped to less than 10 per cent of the total tonnage.

Three-fourths of the nation's iron ore passed across Lake Superior on its way to the steel mills of the southern Great Lakes region. Demand increased for larger ships, and the shipping industry adjusted rapidly to these new realities. Door County, which had been in the mainstream of Great Lakes development, began to be passed by. Timber resources were dwindling and the demand for stone and ice was dropping.

However, even though most of the larger shipping interests on the Great Lakes no longer moved in Door County waters, it was still necessary to transport products, people, and supplies to and from the county. Schooners and wooden steamers, then becoming obsolete, were available at very low cost. Some were converted to barges and continued to be used hauling cargoes throughout the Great Lakes while being towed by the powerful new steamships, but many wooden schooners and smaller steamers were purchased by local entrepreneurs who used them to enter the shipping business on a small, local scale.

Many older ships thus got a reprieve from their ultimate fate and sailed Door County and other Great Lakes waters for many more years. The shipping business run by August and Herman Schuenemann of Ahnapee (now Algoma) used such ships and is one of the best-known examples of a small, family-type shipping operation on the Peninsula.   For over three decades the Schuenemanns shipped thousands of Christmas trees which were harvested in Door County and Upper Michigan to the Chicago market. Over the years their everchanging fleet of ships was made up of old, often leaky, and sometimes downright derelict schooners and lumber hookers for which they usually had paid very little.

The risks of operating a seasonal business combined with sailing any vessel, much less one of questionable seaworthiness, on the Great Lakes in November are obvious.   While the Schuenemanns' enthusiasm, fortitude, and skill at finding their niche in the marketplace are admirable, they each tempted fate once too often. August vanished in the wreck of his thirty-one-year-old, $250 schooner, the *S. Thal* on 9 November 1898 off Glencoe, IL; his brother Herman died in the sinking of the *Rouse Simmons* — the famous forty-four-year-old "Christmas-tree ship" — on 23 November 1911.

Not many of the smaller shippers of Door County suffered the Schuenemanns' tragic fate, but the Schuenemanns' story emphasizes the dangers of Great Lakes navigation and the important role lighthouses have played in preventing calamity for hundreds of other ships.

By the early 1900s, the natural beauty of Door County was becoming recognized by vacationers throughout the Midwest. In this era, tourists began traveling, mainly by water, to many of the ports of Door County, and small and medium-sized passenger ships were built to accommodate this new type of cargo. Such companies as the Hill Line of Fish Creek, the Hart Line of Marinette, and the larger Goodrich Transport Company of Chicago all provided regular service to Door County ports.

36

In 1894, the Ahnapee and Western Railway established service to Sturgeon Bay and began to take a share of the shipping market. The county continually built more and better roads, and, as time went on, motor vehicles were introduced and continued to improve. By the 1930s the romantic era of sailing ships and colorful steam passenger vessels was coming to a close.

However, due to the Ship Canal, Sturgeon Bay continued to thrive as a port of passage between the waters of Green Bay and Lake Michigan, and shipbuilding based in the city of Sturgeon Bay

The *S.S. Arizona*, a passenger and freight steamship of the Goodrich Transport Company which called at Door County ports in the early 1900s.

became the major industry of the county. The shipbuilding industry in Sturgeon Bay is not as robust as it once was, but it is still operating. Many of the enormous modern ore-carriers that comprise today's Great Lakes commercial fleet were built by the Bay Shipbuilding Corporation in Sturgeon Bay, and a sizable portion of the commercial fleet returns there each winter for maintenance and repairs.

The *Cedarville* typified the large, steel Great Lakes freighters that evolved in the early 1900s. Built in 1927, she sank in the Straits of Mackinac in 1965 after a collision with a Norwegian ship in dense fog, a grim reminder that nature will always hold dominion. Lighthouses, foghorns, or other manmade inventions will never be able to entirely prevent maritime tragedy. Door County resident, Francis Felhofer, was one of the divers called on to help recover the bodies of the crewmen that went down with the ill-fated *Cedarville*.

Another type of vessel that has plied Door County waters from the days of the first settlers right down to the present time is the commercial fishing boat. These hardy vessels and crews have been a tradition in Door County for more than 150 years, and they still best represent the rugged image of man against the sea. Commercial fishermen tend their nets in every type of weather in order to supply not only Door County residents and visitors, but people all over the country, with fresh fish for their tables.

The *Margaret* was a commercial fishing vessel, or "fish tug" as they are commonly known, built in 1935 by Peterson Boat Works of Sturgeon Bay, which later became Peterson Builders, Inc. This enclosed, sturdy style of boat is still used by commercial fishermen and is probably the most sea-worthy type of vessel on the Great Lakes.

The first Door County fishing boats were dories; they were built to designs from the European homelands of the fishermen and powered either by wind or by oars. The first steam-powered fishing boat on the peninsula was the *Kitty Gaylord*, put into service on Washington Island in 1870 by the John O'Neill family. This boat was a vast improvement in efficiency and safety over the fishing dory, and it began a revolution in commercial fishing which spread through all of the Great Lakes. The commercial fishing boats of today have incorporated a great deal of the available modern technology, but they also have many similarities in basic design to the *Kitty Gaylord*, built over 125 years ago. They are the most seaworthy craft to sail the waters of Door County.

Today, however, most of the boats that sail in Door County waters are pleasure craft. Many hundreds of them ply in and out of the ports of the Peninsula every summer, and it is primarily for them that Door County lighthouses still fill a vital need.

Lighthouse Administration

Very early in our history, Congress recognized the prime importance of shipping and lighthouses for the growth of the nation; in 1789, they established federal authority over lighthouses by creating the Lighthouse Establishment, administered by the Treasury Department. Responsibility for lighthouse construction and operation and for navigation standards remained with the Treasury Department until 1903.

By 1822 there were seven lighthouses on the Great Lakes, and, with the completion of the Erie Canal, there was a great surge of development from east to west which brought many more ships and lighthouses to the Great Lakes. By 1840 there were forty-three lights on the Lakes including eleven on Lake Michigan; in 1852 there were seventy-six lights on the Great Lakes, with twenty-seven on Lake Michigan, which had the most of any of the Great Lakes.

From 1820 to 1852 the Fifth Auditor of the Treasury, a man named Stephen Pleasanton, was General Superintendent of Lights. A bookkeeper with little knowledge of lighthouses or navigation, Pleasanton had a reputation for being more interested in economy than in effective lighthouse operation or ship safety. Lighthouses were built during his administration, but they were not state-of-the-art lights, and the US lighthouse system began to lag behind those of other nations.

Three of Door County's lighthouses were built during this time period and all suffered from Pleasonton's ineptitude. Pottawatomie Lighthouse (1836) had to be rebuilt in 1858 because the original construction was faulty. The first Porte des Morts Lighthouse (1848) on Plum Island lasted only ten years before it was replaced by a lighthouse on Pilot Island. The reasons could have been poor construction, lack of maintenance, improper location, or a combination of all of these factors. The original

Baileys Harbor Lighthouse (1851) was built in a location that turned out to be less than ideal; it was replaced in 1869.

After an investigation of complaints about lighthouses from all over the United States, the Congress created a nine-member Lighthouse Board in 1852 that was charged with managing the US lighthouse system. During the period from 1852 to 1910, all thirteen of Door County's lighthouses were constructed, rebuilt, or replaced; nationally, the Lighthouse Board was able to turn the system around and make it the best in the world, both in terms of technology and of standards of operation. By 1900 there were 334 major lights, 67 fog signals, and 563 navigation buoys in operation on the Great Lakes.

In 1903, Congress transferred responsibility for the lighthouse system from the Treasury Department to the newly created Department of Commerce & Labor. At that time, many people believed that the lighthouse system ought to be overseen by a single person, and in 1910, Congress abolished the nine-member Lighthouse Board and created the Bureau of Lighthouses, headed by George Putnam. Under Putnam's guidance, the system continued to flourish and expand. The lighthouse system became the responsibility of the US Coast Guard in 1939, and it remains a part of the Coast Guard to this day.

Lighthouses of Death's Door
& the Washington Island Area

Pottawatomie Lighthouse (1837)

Location: The north shore of Rock Island, northeast of Washington Island.
   45 deg. 25 min. 39.5 sec N. latitude
   86 deg. 49 min. 43.5 sec W. longitude

Viewing: Rock Island is a State Park and the grounds (but not the interior of the lighthouse) are open to the public. A State Park daily or seasonal sticker is required. The Washington Island Ferry Line carries both cars & passengers from Northport to Washington Island, then the passenger ferry *Karfi* takes visitors back and forth between Rock Island and Jackson Harbor on the northeast corner of Washington Island. No vehicles are allowed on Rock Island, and it is about a one-mile hike to the lighthouse from the ferry dock.

Summary History:
   – Construction of original lighthouse begun 1836, completed 1837, opened 1838.
   – Lighthouse completely rebuilt 1858 due to faulty construction materials.
   – Steps and platform at bottom of cliff for landing supplies built, 1880.
   – Well drilled at lighthouse, 1910.
   – Entered in National Register of Historic Places, 1979
   – Lantern and lens replaced with automated light, early 1980s.
   – New 41-foot steel light tower replaced lighthouse beacon, 1989.
   – Preservation work to restore lantern room and buildings, 1990s.

Construction & Design: Originally, a 30-foot stone tower with a separate 1½-story stone keepers dwelling, built in 1836–37. However, in 1858 a new stone structure was built; it had 2½-stories, with a tile roof and a square light tower, 8 feet on a side, projecting through the roof.

Tower Height: About 40 feet on the 1858 building.

Height of Light Above Water: About 140 feet on the 1858 building; the current light on a steel tower has its focal plane 159 feet above the water.

Light Type:
   1836 — 11 oil lamps and 11 parabolic reflectors.
   1858 — 9-sided cast-iron lantern, 4th Order Fresnel lens, 14 mile range.

Administration: Grounds and buildings maintained by Rock Island State Park; active steel light tower maintained by US Coast Guard.

Pottawatomie Lighthouse

Construction of the Pottawatomie Lighthouse was begun in 1836, and the light was put into service in 1838. It is the oldest lighthouse in Door County and was the first one built in Wisconsin. It stands on a bluff on the north shore of Rock Island, northeast of Washington Island.

The function of the Pottawatomie Lighthouse is to mark the Rock Island Passage between Rock Island and St Martin's Island to the north. The Rock Island Passage was part of the main route for ships traveling from the eastern Great Lakes to the city of Green Bay, which at that time was the fastest developing city in Wisconsin. The light shone out from its position about 140 feet above the waters of the Rock Island Passage and was visible from a great distance.

The first keeper of the Pottawatomie Lighthouse was a man named David Corbin. He had to carry all his water and supplies from the other side of the island, more than a mile away, because of the high cliffs immediately below the light. Corbin's outpost was isolated, but he did have some opportunity for human contact at a fishing village established on Rock Island in 1837. Corbin remained as keeper of the Pottawatomie Lighthouse until his death in 1852; he is buried on the island near the light.

The original cost of the Pottawatomie Lighthouse is unknown, but the government apparently did not get a good bargain; due to poor construction materials and the destructive effects of nature, the original Pottawatomie Lighthouse was torn down and rebuilt in 1858. The fishing village remained on the island until about 1880, and for many years the basement of the lighthouse served as a schoolroom for the children of Rock Island with the wife of an assistant lighthouse keeper as teacher. Over the years, improvements made life easier for the keepers; in 1880 a landing platform and steps up the cliff were built, and a well was drilled on the site in 1910.

The Pottawatomie Lighthouse was manned and remained in operation until the early 1980s. At that time, a fully automated light on a steel tower was built nearby to replace the old light. Rock Island is a Wisconsin State Park, and the grounds — though not the inside of the building — are open to the public.

The Second Pottawatomie Lighthouse (1858)

To visit the Pottawatomie Lighthouse, visitors must travel to the end of the Door Peninsula, ride two ferries, and hike a mile across Rock Island to the lighthouse site. The trip is well worth the effort. The lighthouse is an historic building of considerable interest in itself, and the site offers an unusual opportunity to experience firsthand the sense of isolation that once characterized most of Door County's lighthouses.

The first Pottawatomie Lighthouse lasted only a little over 20 years because of faulty construction. However, when it was rebuilt in 1858 it was made to last. This view of the upper portion of the building shows the massive stone walls, over a foot thick, and the double-brick arched attic window. Since a group of preservationists has worked to restore the lantern room, the structure now looks almost the same as it did a century and a half ago.

The First Plum Island Lighthouse (1848)

Location: About 1/4 mile east of the Plum Island Rear Range Light on Plum Island in the Death's Door passage between the Door Peninsula and Washington Island. This light is not now active.

Approx 45 deg. 18 min. N. latitude

Approx 86 deg. 57 min. W. longitude

Viewing: The lighthouse ruins on Plum Island are in the interior of the island and are not visible from the water. Plum Island currently is under federal jurisdiction and is off-limits to visitors, so there is no way to view the lighthouse remains.

Summary History:
- Built (known as Port des Morts Lighthouse), 1848; cost unknown.
- Visitor reports lighthouse in bad repair, 1857.
- Equipment dismantled and moved to Pilot Island Light, by 1858.
- Robert Noble stranded on Plum Island overnight in bitter cold in lighthouse ruins consisting of only cellar and chimney, 1 Jan 1864.

Construction/Design: Stone structure with attached kitchen room; little else known.

Tower Height: Unknown.

Height of Light Above Water: Unknown.

Light Type: Probably oil or alcohol lamp with a parabolic reflector, since Fresnel lenses were not yet being used.

Administration: Originally administered by the Lighthouse Establishment under authority of US Treasury Department, Stephen Pleasonton, General Superintendent of Lights. The site on Plum Island is now under Federal jurisdiction.

The First Plum Island Lighthouse

About a quarter mile to the east of the present Plum Island Rear Range Light are the overgrown remains of a building which was once the first *Porte des Morts* Lighthouse. This was only the second lighthouse to be built in Door County; it was constructed in 1848 in an effort to make the Death's Door passage between Washington Island and the tip of the Door County peninsula safer for maritime traffic.

The project made sense — Plum Island lies at about the middle of the northern margin of the Death's Door passage, and ships traveling between Green Bay and ports in southern Lake Michigan could save many miles of travel by using Death's Door instead of the Rock Island passage further to the north. However, as its name implies, *Porte des Morts*, or Death's Door, can be a dangerous place.

Actually, very little is known of this early lighthouse, and it had a very short life; in particular, there is no known contemporary drawing or photograph of the lighthouse. The following account of the first *Porte des Morts* lighthouse is from a 1930 publication of the Door County Historical Society:

> Fortunately we have in Sawyer a person who remembers it very well. Mrs. R. M. Harris, who came with her father, Daniel H. Rice, to Rowleys Bay in 1857, says she has been in this lighthouse many times. It was in charge of an old man by the name of Riggin. According to Mrs. Harris old man Riggin was a terrible old savage who frequently used to drink up the alcohol delivered for lighting purposes. When in his cups he is said to have boasted of piracy and other strange and unconven-tional acts. Evidently old man Riggin was quite a Tartar.

This lighthouse must have been old as early as 1857 for Mrs. Harris tells of how the kitchen part fell down about that time and the main building leaked badly. Under these circumstances it is not strange if the keeper levied a toll on the alcohol for the lighthouse.

Reasoning from this account and from the building date of 1848, it seems that the lighthouse may have been badly maintained by the keeper rather than being especially old. Inferior building materials and construction methods probably also contributed to its poor condition in 1857, since we have already noted that the Pottawatomie Lighthouse on Rock Island had to be completely rebuilt in 1858 for those very reasons.

During the years that the *Porte des Morts* lighthouse operated, many ship captains believed that a lighthouse on *Porte du Mort* Island (later called Pilot Island), located a few miles to the southeast of Plum Island, would be more effective, and they seem to have convinced the powers that were. By 1858, the first *Porte des Morts* lighthouse on Plum Island had been dismantled; its equipment was moved to Pilot Island to become the second Death's Door lighthouse.

Even as a darkened ruin, however, the first Plum Island Lighthouse helped to save the life of one more ill-fated mariner. On 31 December 1863 Robert Noble, now a very well-known early Door County citizen, became stranded on Plum Island while attempting to cross the ice-choked waters of the Death's Door passage in his rowboat.

After a series of misadventures, he spent part of a bitterly cold New Year's Eve in the tumble-down lighthouse ruins. He was able to start a fire in the old fireplace, but it was put out by half-melted snow falling down the old chimney, and he nearly froze to death trying to make his way back to Washington Island. He survived, however, and the story of his adventure that night has become part of Door County lore; it is told in full in the chapter of

Hjalmar Holand's *Old Peninsula Days* called "A Man of Iron: A Tale of Death's Door," as well as in a similar chapter in Holand's twp-volume *History of Door County, Wisconsin.*

Plum Island Range Lights (1896)

Location: On the western and southern sides of Plum Island in the Death's Door passage.

> 45 deg. 18 min. 28.3 sec. N. Latitude
> 86 deg. 57 min. 28.1 sec. W. Longitude

Viewing: There currently is no public access to Plum Island, but the lighthouse can be viewed from the air, from the Washington Island passenger and car ferries, or from private boats.

Summary History:
- Built Aug–Dec 1896 at cost of $21,000; opened 1 May 1897.
- Front Range Light replaced by steel tower, 1964.
- Lights automated, 1969.
- Fog signal removed, 1975.
- Entered in National Register of Historic Places, 1984.

Construction/Design: Rear Plum Island Range Light was constructed of iron and steel, with a pipe and cable framework supporting a cylindrical tower topped by an octagonal platform, a cylindrical watch room, and an octagonal iron lantern room; the Front Plum Island Range Light originally was of wood construction with a square first-story base, and an octagonal second story, located 1650 feet southeast of the rear light. A red-brick steam fog signal building was built ¼-mile north of the rear light, and a 2-story brick keepers' dwelling was placed near the rear light. Wooden walkways connected the lights and the fog signal building.

Tower Height: Rear tower, 65 feet; original front tower about 21 feet; new steel front tower about 30 feet.

Height of Light Above Water: Rear light, 80-foot focal plane; front light originally 32-foot focal plane; new front light 41-foot focal plane.

Light Type: Rear light, 8-sided cast-iron lantern, 4th Order Fresnel lens, range 13 miles, 231 degree visibility arc; front light, 6th Order Fresnel lens, 8½-mile range. The lights are powered by a commercial electric cable running under water for a distance of 8750 feet from Northport on the mainland to Plum Island.

Administration: US Coast Guard

The Plum Island Range Lights

After the first Plum Island Lighthouse was shut down and the equipment moved to Pilot Island in 1858, Plum Island remained without a navigational beacon for almost forty years. The Pilot Island light which replaced it was an improvement, especially for ships traveling from Lake Michigan into Green Bay. However, Death's Door remained a very dangerous passage, and sailing west to east from Green Bay through Death's Door to Lake Michigan was extremely difficult. In particular, the waters near Plum Island and the shoals around it were very hazardous.

Finally, after many years of shipwrecks and close calls in Death's Door, recommendations for a set of range lights on Plum Island were approved, and, by 1897 the Plum Island Range Lights were built, along with a fog signal and a lifesaving station. The rear range light reflected the technology of the day and was constructed of iron and steel. A strip of land 200 feet wide was cleared along the shore, and the front range light was positioned about 1650 feet southeast of the rear light. It was built of wood and was similar in design to the front range light at Baileys Harbor. The new range lights provided a course guide for ships entering Death's Door from Lake Michigan, and the sixty-five-foot rear range tower was visible to ships passing from Green Bay to Lake Michigan, and thus marked Plum Island for them. Martin Knudsen was transferred from Pilot Island to become the first Plum Island Range Light keeper.

The Plum Island Range Lights are still in operation. However, the lights are now fully automated; the front light was replaced by a steel tower in 1964, and the lifesaving station has moved to Washington Island. The Coast Guard has removed the rest of its equipment from the island.

Plum Island is not currently accessible to visitors, but a good view of it can be had either from a private boat or from the ferries which travel back and forth between the mainland and Washington Island.

Plum Island Rear Range Light (1897)

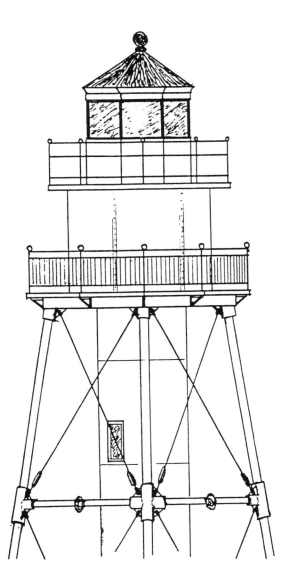

By the 1890s lighthouses were being constructed of iron and steel. This view of the Plum Island Rear Range Light, built in 1897, shows the steel tower, the watch room, and the lantern room which are supported by a system of pipes and cables.

Pilot Island Lighthouse (1858)

Location: About 2 miles east of Northport in Lake Michigan.
45 deg. 17 min. 3.1 sec. N. Latitude
86 deg. 55 min. 11.0 sec. W. Longitude

Viewing: The island is off limits to the general public but the lighthouse can be viewed from the water and a distant view can be had from the Washington Island ferries and tour boats or from shore on the northeast tip of the Door Peninsula.

Summary History:
- Built 1858.
- First fog signal installed, 1864.
- Steam siren fog signal replaced first fog signal, 1875.
- Name of island changed from *Port du Mort* to Pilot Island, 1875.
- Another steam fog signal added in separate building, 1880.
- New landing pier and boathouse constructed, 1891.
- Schooner *A.P. Nichols* wrecked on Pilot Island; keeper Martin Knudsen and assistant Hans Hansen rescue ship's crew, 28 October 1892.
- Steam fog signals replaced by compressed air system, & keepers' quarters enlarged to accommodate assistants and families 1904.
- Fog signal removed and lighthouse automated, 1962.
- Entered in National Register of Historic Places, 1983.

Construction & Design: The Pilot Island Lighthouse originally was a tan brick, two-story keeper's dwelling with a square light tower projecting through the gable roof.

Tower Height: About 35 feet.

Height of Light Above Water: 48-foot focal plane.

Light Type: 10-sided cast-iron lantern, 4th Order Fresnel lens, 11 mile range.

Administration: US Coast Guard.

The Pilot Island Lighthouse

The Pilot Island Lighthouse may have the most dramatic history of any of the Door County lighthouses. Its old log books are full of stories of storms, shipwrecks, rescues, and close calls.

As we have just mentioned, the second Death's Door lighthouse was built in 1858 on the tiny, exposed island that then was called *Port du Mort* Island; the name of both island and lighthouse was changed to Pilot Island in 1875. Located two miles east of modern Northport in Lake Michigan, Pilot Island is near the eastern entrance to Death's Door. It replaced the first Death's Door lighthouse, which had been on Plum Island from 1848 until 1858.

Pilot Island Lighthouse (1858)

The Pilot Island Lighthouse and fog signal were the only sources of navigational aid to ships passing through Death's Door from 1858 until 1897 — a period of time that encompassed the rise and climax of the Great Lakes schooner era.

Schooners were the most beautiful of all Great Lakes ships, but they were also among the most vulnerable, since they relied solely on the fickle winds for propulsion. Even the staunchest vessels and most skilled captains could fall victim to the hazardous currents, shoals, fog, and storms of Death's Door.

Pilot Island epitomizes the image of isolation associated with lighthouses and the keepers who tended them. When weather was good, the keepers and their families often were able to row to the mainland in order to visit friends and to get mail and supplies. Also, the island was a popular destination for adventurous friends and visitors so that, depending upon the season and the weather, keepers and their families might have occasional visitors. But, bad weather or fog might cut them off from the outside world at any time, with very little notice, and an extended period of unfavorable conditions might isolate them completely. Being cut off from other people often evokes strong reactions and feelings. On 4 July 1874 lighthouse keeper Victor Rohn wrote:

> Independence Day came in fine after a heavy southeast gale. This island affords about as much independence and liberty as Libby Prison, with the difference of guards in favor of this place, and chance for outside communication in favor of the other.

A considerably brighter point of view was expressed by a man named Ben Fagg who wrote the following in the *Door County Advocate* in 1890:

The lantern room and equipment of the Pilot Island Lighthouse reportedly came from the first Plum Island Lighthouse, which was dismantled in 1858, the year the Pilot Island light was built. This view of the old lantern room shows the more modern additions of a radio antenna, and a back-up light mounted a post. Many of Door County's lighthouses are equipped with similar lights which automatically turn on if the main light fails.

This is truly an isolated spot but I have spent five days on Pilot Island and they are among the happiest days of my eventuality. . . . One seems to be completely separated from all that is worldly and bad. . . . it is a splendid place to raise an ample crop of good, pure thoughts.

However, it might be pointed out that Mr. Fagg had been on Pilot Island for five days before writing his remarks, while Mr. Rohn had been there several years when he wrote his.

The demands on the keepers of Pilot Island were high. By the early 1900s housing facilities had been expanded to accommodate a keeper, two assistants, and their families. Along with maintaining the light and fog signals, the keepers were occasionally called on to rescue stranded mariners from shipwrecks.

One of the most celebrated keepers of the Pilot Island Lighthouse was Martin Knudsen. He was responsible for saving many lives while stationed at Pilot Island, and he was awarded medals for bravery and outstanding service for one particularly daring rescue. The story of Knudsen's feat is told poetically by William H. Olson, complete with poetic license in the spelling of his name, in the following poem:

Martin Knudson
(or The Lighthouse Keeper's Tale)

As slowly through the field of ice
The island ferry moved
They asked the lighthouse keeper twice
To tell a tale approved.

His eyes lit up, and then they cleared
As he began to tell
About what sailors often feared
Might send them down to hell.

Twas during a November gale
In eighteen ninety-two
When Pilot Island's light would fail
To help the *Nichols'* crew.

The *Nichols'* anchor could not keep
Her from the rocks near shore,
But Martin Knudson did not sleep
That night amid Death's Door.

For Martin, keeper of the light
Knew Pilot's shore by heart,
So out along a shoal that night
To rescue he must start.

Through water almost to his neck
On slippery rocks he went,
For if he could not reach the wreck
Its fate was evident.

He asked them to abandon ship
He'd catch them as they leapt.
As climax to this risky trip
All six he'd intercept.

He piloted the crew ashore
Along a crooked shoal
And safe behind the lighthouse door
Which was there sheltered goal.

Another ship, the *Gilmore*, too
Fetched up off Pilot's light
So sixteen men must all make do
On rations very tight.

From *Nichols'* wreck they salvaged fare
And all rode out the storm
For one more week in Martin's care
Quite snug and dry and warm.

(From *Island Verse*, by William H. Olson)

      The Pilot Island Lighthouse was automated in 1962, and its fog signal was removed at that time. Today, without the human presence formerly provided by keepers and their families, the isolation of Pilot Island seems complete. There is no access for visitors to the island, though it can be viewed from an airplane or boat, and it can also be seen in the distance from the Washington Island Ferry or from the eastern shore of the tip of the Door Peninsula. Seen in the evening as night is falling, the solitude of the place becomes even more profound as the lonely light takes up its silent vigil, still providing a visual fixed point to help captains guide their boats through the Death's Door Passage.

An artist's conception of Martin Knudsen in the act of rescuing a crewman from the *A.P. Nichols*. The drawing is based on William Olson's poem "Martin Knudson (or the Lighthouse Keeper's Tale)" from his book *Island Verse*.

Lighthouses on the Lake Michigan Side of the Door

Old Baileys Harbor Lighthouse (1851)

Location: East of the village of Baileys Harbor on a small island near the harbor entrance. This light is not now active.

      Approx. 45 deg. 4 min. N. latitude

      Approx. 87 deg. 7 min. W. longitude

Viewing: The island is private and is inaccessible to visitors, but the lighthouse tower can be viewed from the water or from land at the end of Ridges Road.

Summary History:
- Village of Baileys Harbor founded 1848; lighthouse built 1851.
- Replaced by Baileys Harbor Range Lights 1869.

Construction/Design: The lighthouse tower is constructed of stone. It is round and tapers upward. Towers of this style have walls several feet thick at the base that get progressively thinner toward the top. A stone keeper's dwelling was built adjacent to the tower.

Tower Height: about 40 feet.

Light Type: Bird cage style lantern, probably oil lamp(s) with parabolic reflector(s).

Administration: Currently privately owned

The Old Baileys Harbor Lighthouse

When Alanson Sweet began the village of Baileys Harbor in 1848 he wasted little time in petitioning for a lighthouse to be built to guide the large number of ships he envisioned entering his new port.

The Old Baileys Harbor Lighthouse (1851)

By 1851 the lighthouse was completed on a small island on the east side of the entrance to the harbor, but the light was in use only until 1869. The many shoals off the eastern harbor shore made entry to the harbor difficult and dangerous. It was decided that a set of range lights closer to the village on the northwest side of the harbor would be much more useful. This decision was made, in part, because in addition to being a port of destination for many ships Baileys Harbor was considered the only safe harbor on the western shore of Lake Michigan north of Milwaukee where ships could seek refuge during bad weather.

The forty foot round tower of the abandoned lighthouse is constructed of stone. It is unique in that it had what was known as a "bird cage" lantern room. There reportedly are only three bird cage lighthouses known still to exist in the United States. The tall, narrow, domed metal framework of the lantern room is still visible above the trees that have grown up around the lighthouse. The island on which it stands is private and the only good view of the deteriorating structure from land is at the end of Ridges Road. The historical significance and unusual design of the lighthouse would make it a good candidate for restoration and preservation.

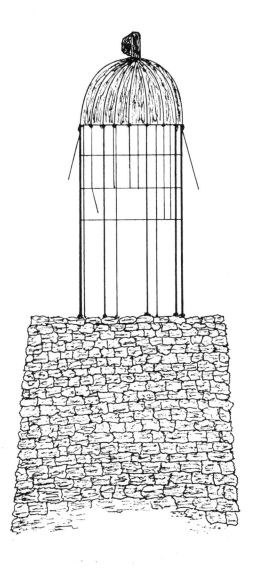

The deteriorating stone tower of the Old Baileys Harbor Lighthouse supports the remains of a "bird cage" lantern. There are very few remaining lanterns of this type. By the 1860s this tall, delicate-looking style had been replaced by the sturdier polygonal lanterns seen on most of Door County's lighthouses.

Baileys Harbor Range Lights (1869)

Location: In the Ridges Sanctuary at Baileys Harbor.
   45 deg. 4 min. 11.3 sec. N. latitude
   87 deg. 7 min. 9.8 sec. W. longitude

Viewing: The entrance to the Ridges Sanctuary is just off Highway 57 on County Road Q at the north end of Baileys Harbor. Call the Ridges Sanctuary for hours and fee information. The Range Light buildings are not open to the public but can be closely viewed from the hiking trails and the restored boardwalk linking the lights. The Range Lights can also be viewed from Ridges Road, but the Ridges Sanctuary administration prefers that visitors use the main entrance.

Summary History:
   – Built Summer & Fall 1869 at cost of $6,000; opened Spring 1870.
   – Automated, lights converted to acetylene gas, 1923.
   – Lights converted to electricity, 1930.
   – Deeded to Door County Park Commission, 1934.
   – Lighting equipment removed & replaced by 30-foot steel light tower near front range light, 1969.
   – Entered in National Register of Historic Places, 1989.

Construction & Design: Wood frame construction. The rear light tower was built into the 1½-story keeper's dwelling and projects above gabled roof; the front tower has a square base and an octagonal upper section; the front and rear lights are 950 feet apart, connected by a 600-foot wooden boardwalk.

Tower Height: Rear tower, 35 feet; front tower, 21 feet.

Height of Light Above Water: Rear light, 39-foot focal plane; front light, 22-foot focal plane.

Light Type: Rear light, 5th Order Fresnel lens, 13 mile range; front light, Steamer lens, 11 mile range.

Administration: Owned by Door County and leased to the Ridges Sanctuary; US Coast Guard maintains the steel light tower.

Baileys Harbor Range Lights

Nestled among the rare boreal plant life of the Ridges Sanctuary, the Baileys Harbor Range Lights create a harmonious blend of the manmade and natural.

More sheltered from the elements than other Door County lighthouse locations, the Range Lights are of wooden construction rather than the typical stone or brick.

Baileys Harbor Range Lights (1869)

The Baileys Harbor Range Lights were built in 1869 as a more effective replacement for the original Baileys Harbor Lighthouse. The 21-foot front light is near the shore about 950 feet in front of the keeper's residence and attached rear light tower. The rear light is about 39 feet above Lake Michigan. A 600-foot boardwalk spans the swampy area between the two lights.

Ship captains found safe entrance to the harbor by lining up the taller rear light directly over the front light, knowing that if they followed this course their vessels would avoid reefs, shoals, and rocky shores.

In 1923 the lights were automated and the keeper transferred to Cana Island Lighthouse. The keeper maintained the Range Lights through periodic visits and the Range Light keeper's house stood vacant for several years. In 1930 the lights were converted to electric power, and from then until 1955 the building was used as a parsonage by Lutheran pastors and their families.

In 1937 the Ridges Sanctuary was organized. The lighthouse property, which had been deeded to the Door County Park Commission in 1934, is now under lease to the Ridges. All of the lighthouse buildings are on the National Register of Historic Places and the Sanctuary has done extensive restoration to the lights and boardwalk.

The lights are no longer active. In 1969 a steel light tower was built nearby to replace the Range Lights. Visitors are requested to view the lights by using the Ridges Sanctuary entrance on County Road Q. There is no access to the interiors of the buildings but a close view can be had from the hiking trails and boardwalk. The Range Lights are also visible from Ridges Road.

Looking more like a country schoolhouse than a lighthouse, the Baileys Harbor Rear Range Light is the only Door County lighthouse to have a gable roofed wooden lantern room. It is built into the wood frame keeper's house and has a single window through which it's beacon was cast down range above the lower Front Range Light, guiding ships on a deep water passage from Lake Michigan into Baileys Harbor.

Cana Island Lighthouse (1869)

Location: Approximately 5 miles northeast of Baileys Harbor.
45 deg. 5 min. 17.2 sec. N. Latitude
87 deg. 2 min. 51.5 sec. W. Longitude

Viewing: Take county road Q off HWY 57 just north of Baileys Harbor. Travel about 3.5 miles to Cana Island Road and follow this road to its end. The island is maintained by the Door County Maritime Museum and visitors are welcome. Call the Maritime Museum for hours and fee information. Cross to the island on foot via the causeway. However, note that at times of high water the causeway may be under water and wading may be necessary. The keeper's dwelling is open to the public, but not the light tower.

Summary History:
- Built 1869; opened 24 January 1870; cost unknown.
- Cana Island and lighthouse flooded by storms, 1870s and 1880s.
- Low areas of island filled in, 1890.
- Tower encased in steel plates 1902.
- Gravel causeway connecting island to shore built during WW I.
- Island leased by Door County Maritime Museum from the Federal Government, 1970s.
- Entered in National Register of Historic Places, 1976.

Construction/Design: The Cana Island Lighthouse has a keepers' dwelling built of tan-colored brick and measuring 42 feet by 27 feet and a tower that is some 18 feet in diameter at its base. A brick passage connects the tower and dwelling. The tower was later sheathed in riveted steel plates; there is a brick watch room on top of tower.

Tower Height: Approximately 88 feet to top of ventilator ball.

Height of Light Above Water: 83-foot focal plane.

Light Type: 10-sided cast-iron lantern with a 3rd Order Fresnel lens, 17 mile range.

Administration: Door County Maritime Museum; the active, automated light is maintained by US Coast Guard.

Cana Island Lighthouse

The Cana Island Lighthouse was built in 1869. It has an impressive 88-foot tower, and it stands boldly on the east side of Cana Island north of Baileys Harbor. A low hand built stone wall and rocky beach are all that separate it from Lake Michigan. The light marks the rocky and shallow shoreline and helped ships to find safe refuge in North Bay to the north and Moonlight Bay to the south.

Cana Island Lighthouse (1869)

The island, just off shore, has a rock bridge causeway that can be crossed on foot when the water and waves are not too high. Visitors have remarked on the astounding beauty of the place. Ida Margaret Bay, Door County historian and long time antique dealer, was one of the leading advocates and forces behind Door County lighthouse preservation. In an article published in 1958 by the Door County Historical Society she wrote,

> None but a poet could adequately describe the beautiful little island . . . . What a spot for an artist, a writer or just a dreamer! How difficult to separate reality from the realm of fancy in this place!

Mother Nature, however, is not always so kind, and when the occasional eastern squall kicks up serenity turns to a more rugged beauty, both harsh and violent. Such a storm befell W. Sanderson, the lighthouse keeper, and his family on the evening of 15 October 1880. Bay describes the incident:

> Giant waves frequently broke over the house and the spray reached to the very top of the 83 foot tower. The lantern at times was completely covered with water. The thick plate glass finally was broken by the force.

> So great was the vibration that the iron stair to the tower was pulled away from the wall.

> During the first night of the storm the light-house keeper stayed in the tower all night. His family decided to remain in the house as long as possible. But when the water reached a height of three feet in the kitchen they were forced to leave.

> With nothing more than a lantern, a blanket and a pan of corn bread they stepped into the

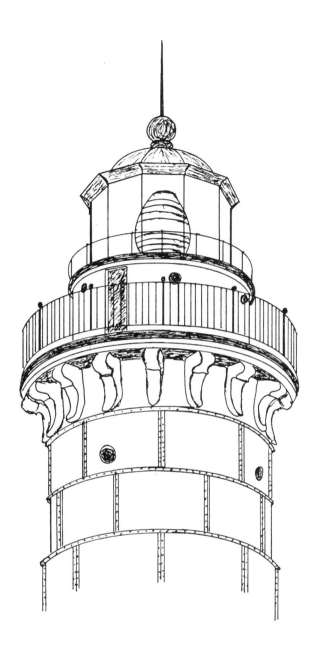

The tall brick light tower of Cana Island Lighthouse was wrapped in a protective sheath of riveted steel plates in 1902 after the ravages of Door County weather began to weaken and threatened to destroy the landmark structure. The original ornate platform and brick watch room still support the lantern and its powerful Third Order Fresnel lens.

swirling waters and the howling darkness of a night they would always remember.

In a matter of seconds the lantern was useless. Painfully and ever so slowly they groped their way through icy water, mud, rocks and underbrush. Finally they reached the west side of the island and found shelter in the small boathouse there. Chilled and very wet they spent the rest of that miserable night huddled in the bottom of a rowboat while the storm grew steadily worse.

Two more days and nights were spent in the same manner. On the third day after the storm had subsided somewhat the children rowed about the island in a small skiff . . . peeking into windows they could never reach before and viewing the devastation within.

After this and other bad storms low areas of the island were filled in to help prevent flooding. One of the keepers, Oscar Knudson, built the stone wall around the lighthouse. In 1902 the brick light tower was encased in steel plate to protect it from the storms of Lake Michigan.

Cana Island Lighthouse, now fully automated, is maintained by the Coast Guard but the island was leased to the Door County Maritime Museum in the 1970's for the purpose of historical preservation. The grounds around the lighthouse and the keeper's residence are open to the public but there is no access to the light tower.

Lighthouses on the Green Bay Side of the Door

Chambers Island Lighthouse (1868)

Location: Northwest corner of Chambers Island about 8 miles northwest of Fish Creek.

  45 deg. 12 min. 6.4 sec. N. Latitude
  87 deg. 21 min. 56.3 sec. W. Longitude

Viewing: There is no public boat service to take passengers to the island, but the lighthouse can be viewed from the water on private boats. The grounds of the lighthouse are open to the public during the day. When the caretakers are there they will be happy to give you a tour of the lighthouse building, but there are no regular visiting hours at this time. Joel and Mary Ann Blahnik are the caretakers and they are currently establishing a lighthouse museum at the site.

Summary History:
- Built summer 1868 at cost of $9,000; opened 1 Oct 1868
- Lighthouse closed & replaced with automated 97-foot steel tower, 1961.
- Entered in National Register of Historic Places, 1975.
- Lighthouse and grounds transferred to Town of Gibraltar, 1976.
- Joel and Mary Ann Blahnik caretakers since 1976, working summers to restore facilities and create a museum.

Construction & Design: The Chambers Island Lighthouse buildings consist of a 1½-story keepers' dwelling measuring 26 feet by 30 feet, with an attached kitchen measuring 12 feet by 20 feet, and with a attached light tower that has a square bottom half with buttresses, and an octagonal upper section, all built of tan-colored brick.

Tower Height: 45 feet.

Height of Light Above Water: 68-foot focal plane.

Light Type: Cast-iron 10-sided lantern, 4th Order Fresnel lens, 16-mile range.

Administration: Town of Gibraltar; US Coast Guard maintains steel light tower.

Chambers Island Lighthouse

The Chambers Island Lighthouse was built in 1868 on a finger of land on the northwest corner of the island. Its main purpose was to mark the island and the western main channel used by ships traveling to the city of Green Bay.

Chambers Island Lighthouse (1868)

The lighthouse stands on a 40-acre parcel of land which the government purchased for $250 from Lewis and Anna Williams in 1867. Williams must have been a good negotiator because he also landed the job of lighthouse keeper and served in that position until 1889.

The brick light tower has a unique design, square in shape on the bottom half and becoming octagonal on the top half. It was built this way so that the lighthouse would look different than nearby Eagle Bluff Lighthouse which is almost identical except for a full square light tower. During daylight hours ship captains often used the distinctive shapes of lighthouses as a reference to pinpoint their ship's location.

The Coast Guard took over operation of the lighthouse in 1939. In 1961 a fully automated steel light tower on the grounds replaced the original light.

In 1976 the Town of Gibraltar obtained possession of the old lighthouse and grounds. Joel and Mary Ann Blahnik became the official caretakers of the property and are currently reconstructing the past as they assemble the Chambers Island Lighthouse Museum.

The Blahniks have had many interesting experiences during their years at the lighthouse. One story that Joel tells is that of the ghost that haunted the lighthouse when he first began spending summers there as caretaker:

> I was opening the place for the first time in the season. My son and I spent the day tidying up. We went to bed that night and, enjoying the island's peaceful silence, drifted into sleep.
>
> Soon, however, I was awakened by the sound of heavy footsteps coming down the cast iron spiral staircase of the light tower, booming through

The architectural design of the brick Chambers Island light tower is reminiscent of a castle or cathedral. This drawing illustrates the buttressed supports on the square tower base which becomes octagonal in shape in the top half of the tower. The whole structure is built into a corner of the keeper's dwelling.

the quiet lighthouse. I lay frozen in my bed, my hair standing on end. I called out to my son who would not wake up from his sleep. The footsteps proceeded from the tower to the hall, across the living room, through the kitchen, and out the door with a clear snap of the latch as the door closed.

In the morning I tried to imagine what could have happened the night before, but I came up with nothing. The ghost did not bother us for the rest of the season.

However, when opening up the lighthouse the next season, I had a similar experience. On the first night I heard the footsteps starting on the tower stairs and walking through the house and out the door. I speculated that this occurrence could be the result of a ghost who was a former lighthouse keeper. When I showed up it seemed that the old ghostly keeper would come down out of the lighthouse and leave it to me for the summer season.

Once renovation of the lighthouse began in earnest the ghost began doing more than graciously leaving the premises once I arrived. The more work I did on the place the more mischievous the ghost became. Tools would disappear and show up in the most unlikely spots. The local people on the island and back in Fish Creek heard about this. Skeptical visitors who spent the night were often haunted. Sometimes their beds would shake as if by a mighty, unseen pair of hands.

One day, a priest from the Holy Name Retreat House was entertaining some visiting nuns for a picnic at the lighthouse. The priest mentioned the ghost and told of the things it had done. One of the sisters who was moved by these stories put her hands on the building to feel the presence of this trapped soul. She prayed for his release. Since that day the ghost has not made his presence known.

The identity of this ghost has been a matter of speculation. Joel's research into the people who have lived at the lighthouse has uncovered many stories of the difficulties of early lighthouse life, some including great tragedy. One such story is that of a former assistant keeper, Sam Hanson. Hanson had served at the lighthouse from 1906-1913 and then returned to serve again in 1916 as a widower with two sons and two small daughters. In May of 1921 his son Edgar, age 15, suffered an attack of appendicitis and died en route to the Egeland Hospital in Sturgeon Bay in what must have been a long and agonizing journey in the lighthouse's small boat. The following April his son Clifford, 18, fell through the ice while walking across to the mainland and drowned.

However, Joel does not feel that the ghost is from the Hanson family. He thinks that a possible candidate is Jens Rollefson, a Norwegian bachelor who was head keeper for many years and who had died during one winter in his room in Fish Creek while waiting for the new shipping season to begin.

In Joel's opinion, the most likely identity of the ghost is Lewis Williams, the first keeper of the light. Williams had very strong ties to the lighthouse property, having owned it before the lighthouse was built, and he served as keeper there for 21 years, longer than any other keeper.

Access to the lighthouse is limited. The grounds are open to the public during the day but there is no public boat service to the island. The lighthouse can be viewed from private boats. The Blahniks also welcome visitors when they are in residence, but there are no regular hours at this time.

Eagle Bluff Lighthouse (1868)

Location: In Peninsula State Park between Fish Creek and Ephraim.
    45 deg. 10 min. 7.3 sec. N. Latitude
    87 deg. 14 min. 12.0 sec. W. Longitude

Viewing: The main entrance to Peninsula State Park is in Fish Creek; a daily or seasonal State Park sticker is required. From the main entrance, the lighthouse is about four miles north on Shore Road. The Door County Historical Society has completely restored the site and offers guided tours through the buildings. The Peninsula State Park Office (at the main entrance) can furnish information on hours and fees. This is the best opportunity for visitors to experience what life was like in a working lighthouse of the 1800s.

Summary History:
- Built Spring/Summer 1868 at cost of $12,000; opened 15 Oct 1868.
- Lighthouse automated with acetylene gas light, 1926.
- Lighthouse and grounds leased to Peninsula State Park, 1936.
- Door County Historical Society began restoration of site, 1960.
- Lighthouse site opened as museum, September 1963.
- Entered in National Register of Historic Places, 1970.

Construction & Design: The Eagle Bluff Lighthouse consisted of a 1½-story keeper's dwelling measuring 26 feet by 30 feet, with an attached kitchen measuring 12 feet by 20 feet, and a square light tower built onto the corner of dwelling at a 45-degree angle to the rest of the structure. The spiral tower steps were also used as the staircase for the dwelling.

Tower Height: 44 feet.

Height of Light Above Water: 76-foot focal plane.

Light Type: Original (1868) light had a 10-sided cast-iron lantern, with a 3½-Order Fresnel lens, and a 16 mile range; it was changed to a 5th Order Fresnel Lens with a 7-mile range in 1918.

Administration: Lighthouse site is part of Peninsula State Park; the museum is operated by the Door County Historical Society; the active light, now electric, is maintained by US Coast Guard.

Eagle Bluff Lighthouse

Eagle Bluff Lighthouse was built in 1868 on a cliff overlooking the waters of Green Bay in what is now Peninsula State Park. The purpose of the light was to mark the passage between the mainland and the many outlying islands in the area. It helped sailors find their way to the rapidly growing ports of Ephraim to the north and Fish Creek to the south.

Eagle Bluff Lighthouse (1868)

The image that most lighthouses have of isolation and loneliness has never fit Eagle Bluff Lighthouse. From 1868 until its automation in 1926 only three keepers and their families were stationed there and all were well known and liked by people in the area. With its parklike grounds, spectacular view, and sociable families keeping the light, Eagle Bluff saw a steady stream of visitors from nearby Ephraim and Fish Creek.

The first keeper was Henry Stanley. He and his family lived at the light from 1868 until 1883 when Stanley was transferred to the newly built Sherwood Point Lighthouse near Sturgeon Bay.

William Duclon, the second light keeper, brought his wife and seven sons to Eagle Bluff in 1883 and stayed until his retirement in 1918 after 35 years of service at the light. In *Eagle Lighthouse*, Door County writer Frances Badtke wrote, "In a way, the story of the lighthouse is partly the story of the Duclon family". A visit to the Eagle Bluff Lighthouse Museum shows that this is true.

With a wage of thirty dollars a month and some basic supplies Duclon was earning what was considered a good living for that time period. But the Duclons were a pioneer family living in an undeveloped area. There was no supermarket down the street. With seven growing and hungry boys to feed the Duclons depended on what they could provide for themselves. Everyone did their share. William's wife, Julia, grew a large garden and raised chickens and a cow and the boys helped with the chores. The boys all contributed by hunting and fishing.

William, again with the help of the rest of the family, maintained the light and grounds. He was dedicated to this job and over the years received awards of excellence for the neatness and organized operation of the light station.

The ornate turned wood decoration on the gable end of the Eagle Bluff Lighthouse keeper's dwelling is a feature common to many lighthouses on the Great Lakes. It emphasizes the fact that as lighthouses were being built to serve a practical function, their designers also were creating a long-lasting legacy of architectural beauty.

Through their hard work the Duclons carved out a comfortable way of life at Eagle Bluff. Despite the work they also found ample time for more leisurely pursuits. Julia was well-known for creating award winning embroidered quilts. The boys became accomplished musicians. They formed the Duclon Band and were in demand to play at dances in the area villages. All the boys, their instruments, including a Stradivarius violin and even a baby grand piano, were loaded on a sleigh or wagon to travel to performances which often lasted all night.

As the boys grew up, married, and moved off to begin families of their own Eagle Bluff continued to be the hub of the family. The growing clan often gathered at the light station for lively holiday celebrations and family get-togethers.

The Duclons are shining examples of the type of pioneers who made their mark on the early history of Door County. A combination of dedication to responsibility, hard work, independence, and an enjoyment of the people and the place that are the Door Peninsula. Their light still shines over Eagle Bluff.

For a fascinating fictionalized look into the life of the Duclon family in those pioneer days, take a look at the book *Eagle Bluff Journal 1895* by Phyl Mielke.

After Duclon retired Peter Coughlin became keeper. He and his wife carried on the tradition of hospitality as visitors continued to visit Eagle Bluff. In 1926 Coughlin retired and the lighthouse was automated.

Today Eagle Bluff Lighthouse is operated as a museum by the Door County Historical Society. The facility has been totally restored and visitors can step back in time to the days and lives of the lighthouse keepers and their families.

Lighthouses of the
Sturgeon Bay Area

Sturgeon Bay North Pierhead Light (1882)

Location: About 5 miles southeast of the city of Sturgeon Bay on the shore of Lake Michigan at the entrance to the Ship Canal

> 44 deg. 47 min. 31.3 sec N. Latitude
> 87 deg. 18 min. 34.0 sec W. Longitude

Viewing: See Sturgeon Bay Ship Canal Lighthouse.

History:
- Built Summer & Fall, 1881; opened 15 May 1882; cost unknown.
- Sturgeon Bay Ship Canal officially opened 1882.
- Steam-powered fog signal built on North Pier, 1884.
- Second steam fog signal added; keeper's dwelling built on shore, 1886.
- Ship Canal purchased by Federal Government for $103,000, to be operated by US Corps of Engineers, 1893.
- Life-saving station built at site, 1896.
- Ship Canal Lighthouse built on shore, 1898.
- North Pierhead tower & fog signals replaced, 1903.
- Transferred to US Coast Guard administration, 1939.

Construction/Design: The Sturgeon Bay North Pierhead Lighthouse originally was built as an open-framed light tower with separate fog signal buildings on the North Pier; an elevated walkway on the pier ran from shore to buildings. The 1903 structure combined the fog signal and the light tower in a 24-foot by 33-foot building of quarter-inch steel plate.

Tower Height: Original tower about 30 feet; rebuilt tower 39 feet.

Height of Light Above Water: Original light had a 35-foot focal plane; the rebuilt light has a 40-foot focal plane.

Light & Fog Signal Type: Originally equipped with a 10-sided cast-iron lantern and a 6th-Order Fresnel lens; the same equipment was used in the rebuilt structure, current range 9 miles. Originally equipped with 10-inch steam fog whistles, range 8-12 miles; it now has an electric fog signal.

Administration: US Coast Guard.

The Sturgeon Bay North Pierhead Light

The Sturgeon Bay North Pierhead Light and the Sturgeon Bay Ship Canal Lighthouse both exist because of the Ship Canal itself, and they are very close together. The Sturgeon Bay Ship Canal Lighthouse is discussed below beginning on p. 98.

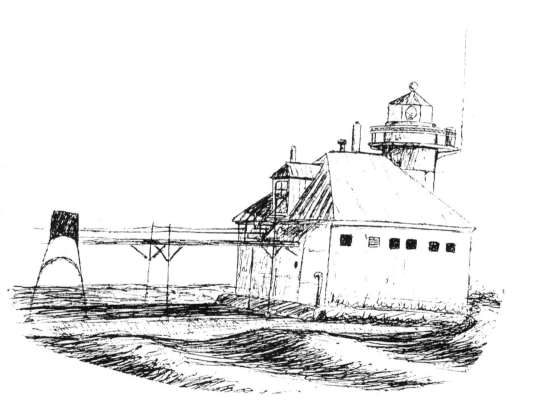

Sturgeon Bay North Pierhead Light (1882)

In the 1860s Joseph Harris Sr., one of Sturgeon Bay's most influential and progressive citizens, first began the long effort to have a canal built linking the waters of Green Bay and Lake Michigan. Long before white settlers came to Sturgeon Bay, Native Americans had portaged their canoes and supplies across the one-mile strip of land that separated the bodies of water on either side of the Peninsula.

In Harris' opinion the canal would serve as a means of quicker, safer, and cheaper transport of lumber from the saw mills of Sturgeon Bay to the developing cities on the Great Lakes by eliminating the passage around the Peninsula and through Death's Door. He also believed that the short cut the canal would offer to any ship traveling between Green Bay waters and the southern Lake Michigan region would make Sturgeon Bay a busy shipping center on this route.

In 1882 Harris and his business partners saw their dream fulfilled as the canal opened to traffic. The predictions of growth for Sturgeon Bay were accurate. During the 1880s and 1890s as many as 7,000 ships per season passed through the canal.

To provide safe entry from Lake Michigan into this new waterway the government commissioned a breakwall, lighthouse, and fog signal to be built. The North Pierhead Light was completed in 1882, in time for the official opening of the Ship Canal; a steam-powered fog signal was added in 1884, and a second fog signal and a keeper's dwelling was built on the site in 1886. A second lighthouse — the Sturgeon Bay Ship Canal Lighthouse — was built on shore behind the Pierhead light; it went into service in 1899, and since then both lights have operated.

The Sturgeon Bay Ship Canal Lighthouse is discussed below, beginning on p. 98.

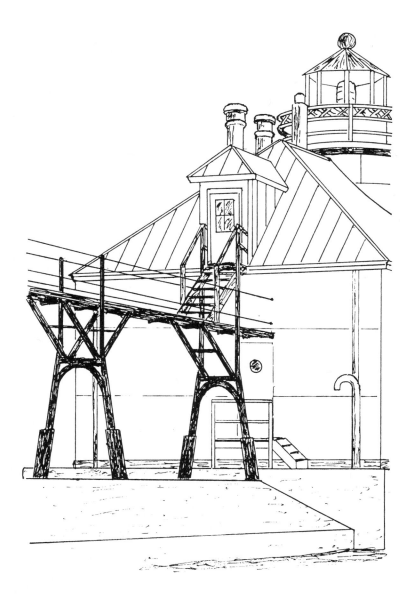

The two breakwater piers at the Lake Michigan entrance to the Sturgeon Bay Ship Canal extend several hundred feet into the lake. The North Pierhead Light is built on the end section of the northern breakwater pier and is separated from the main section of the northern pier by open water. It can be reached only by way of the elevated walkway illustrated above. The walkway allows access to the light even when high waves are breaking over the pier below.

Sturgeon Bay Ship Canal Lighthouse (1899)

Location: Five miles southeast of the city of Sturgeon Bay on the shore of Lake Michigan at the entrance to the Ship Canal.

    44 deg. 47 min. 42.0 sec. N. Latitude
    87 deg. 18 min. 47.6 sec. W. Longitude

Viewing: Go east on Utah Street which intersects Highway 42-57 about half a mile north of the Bay View Bridge. Turn right onto Cove Road then left onto Canal Road which leads to the ship canal and the lighthouses. Access is not permitted to the grounds of the active Coast Guard station (on which the light tower stands), but visitors can get good views of all the facilities from the public path that leads to the breakwater pier. Public parking areas, paths, and viewing areas have also been constructed along the length of the Ship Canal itself.

Summary History:
  – Built 1898 at cost of $20,000; officially opened 17 March 1899.
  – Steel support framework added to correct vibration problem, 1903.
  – Keepers' dwelling enlarged to accommodate additional keepers for Ship
      Canal Light and North Pierhead Light, 1903.
  – Entered in National Register of Historic Places, 1984.

Construction & Design: The tower was built as a steel cylinder 8 feet in diameter set on a concrete base, with eight 16-foot buttresses as support and with a cylindrical watch room and lantern on top of the tower. It apparently was a flawed design, as it experienced severe vibration in high winds; steel truss supports added to the full height of the tower cylinder solved the vibration problem.

Tower Height: 98 feet.

Height of Light Above Water: 107-foot focal plane.

Light Type: Cast-iron lantern with diagonal framework for curved glass panels, 3rd Order rotating Fresnel lens, 17 mile range.

Administration: US Coast Guard.

The Sturgeon Bay Ship Canal Lighthouse

Though the North Pierhead Light (see above, p. 94) was placed in service on this site in 1882, it was not long before shippers expressed a need for a taller, brighter light, and, in 1899, a 98-foot tower was completed on the shore directly behind the North Pierhead first light. The tower was built to a new and somewhat unusual design consisting of a cylinder eight feet in diameter, on top of which sat a watch room and the lantern. The design was flawed, however, and in strong winds the tower vibrated and swayed dangerously. In 1903, it was necessary to add a steel framework surrounding the cylinder and supporting the watch room and the lantern; this extra support finally solved the problem.

Sturgeon Bay Ship Canal Lighthouse (1899)

Although the two lights at the Ship Canal were built at different times and were not designed as a set of range lights, they do, in essence, serve that function. By lining up the taller light in relation to the lower pierhead light mariners are able to guide their ships to the vicinity of the breakwater entrance where smaller lights and lighted bougs guide ships the rest of the way into safe harbor.

The Coast Guard now maintains and operates both lights along with the Life Saving Station which had been built at the Ship Canal in 1896. Visitors may walk down the road and out on the breakwater pier but are not allowed on the grounds of the station. There are also parking areas and access trails along the Ship Canal from which visitors can get a close up view of the hundreds of pleasure boats and occasional commercial ships that still use this manmade short cut into Sturgeon Bay.

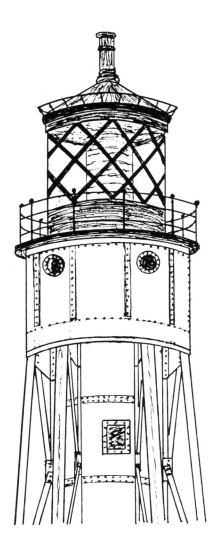

The lantern room of the Sturgeon Bay Ship Canal Light, with its diagonal cast-iron supports and diamond-patterned curved glass panels, is unique among Door County lighthouse designs. It also houses the county's only rotating Third Order Fresnel lens. The steel support framework of the tower was added in 1903 to solve a design flaw which caused the tower to sway dangerously in high winds.

Dunlap Reef Lighthouse (1881)

Location: Formerly located on Dunlap Reef which is now marked by buoys parallel to the ship channel in front of Bay Shipbuilding Corporation in Sturgeon Bay. There is no light on the site at the present time.

> Approx. 44 deg. 50 min. N. latitude
> Approx. 87 deg. 23 min. W. longitude

Viewing: While the lighthouse itself no longer exists, the keeper's dwelling was moved across the ice and is now a private residence at 411 S. 4th Ave. in Sturgeon Bay. It looks much the same today, minus the light tower, as it did when it was part of the lighthouse. It can be viewed from the street only and the residents' privacy should be respected.

Summary History:
- Built 1881 as rear light of set of range lights.
- Sturgeon Bay Ship Canal opened, 1882.
- Sturgeon Bay incorporated 1883, lighthouse and Dunlap Reef became part of the city.
- Lighthouse use discontinued, 1924.
- Keeper's dwelling sold, not including lighting equipment, and building moved across ice to become a private residence, 1925.

Construction/Design: The Dunlap Reef Lighthouse was of wood frame construction; it consisted of a 1½-story keeper's dwelling measuring 23 feet by 25 feet, with a wood light tower inset into the front of the structure, and an attached boathouse on rear of building. A stone crib foundation supported the structures.

Tower Height: Approximately 40 feet from the base of the tower to the top of ventilator ball.

Height of Light Above Water: About 42-foot focal plane.

Light Type: 8-sided cast-iron lantern, lens and range unknown.

Administration: Surviving keeper's dwelling is a private residence.

Dunlap Reef Lighthouse

Dunlap Reef is located in about the middle of Sturgeon Bay, to the west of the old downtown bridge in the city of Sturgeon Bay. Over the years, many vessels have run aground on it, and there once was a full-size lighthouse tower attached to a keeper's house on the site. This lighthouse formed part of a set of range lights that served to guide ships approaching Sturgeon Bay from Green Bay, as well as to mark Dunlap Reef itself. The lighthouse was on one end of the reef, and the other light was 700 feet away at the other end.

Dunlap Reef Lighthouse (1881)

The lighthouse was built in 1881 in anticipation of the increased shipping traffic that would come with the then-soon-to-be-completed Sturgeon Bay Ship Canal. It's close proximity and easy access to the city of Sturgeon Bay made it much sought after as an assignment for lighthouse keepers, and there was little turnover in the keeper's position.

A look down the waters of Sturgeon Bay today shows that the lighthouse is no longer there. In 1924, it was decided that the lighthouse was no longer needed, perhaps because the Sherwood Point Lighthouse and the lights of the growing city of Sturgeon Bay provided sufficient navigational aid to guide ships into the harbor and because the task of marking Dunlap Reef could be done much less expensively by using lighted buoys. A fixed navigational light and a buoy continue to mark the reef today.

The attractive white light tower and wood keeper's dwelling in the bay are now just a memory. The lighthouse is not completely lost to history, however, for when it was dismantled the keeper's house was put on skids, dragged down the bay over the winter ice, and now is a private residence at 411 S. 4th Avenue in the heart of Sturgeon Bay. With its neatly painted white clapboard siding, minus the light tower, the building looks much the same now as it did back in 1881.

The construction style is very similar to many other private residences which were built in the city during the late 1800's and if one did not know its history there would be no clue that it was once a lighthouse. The building can be viewed from the street but the privacy of the residents should be respected. One hopes that the owners will appreciate its historical significance and preserve it for the future, though it is no longer even in view of the bay it once stood watch over.

Dunlap Reef Lighthouse was the only Door County lighthouse with a full-size cast-iron lantern room atop an all-wood tower, shown above. It graced Sturgeon Bay during the late 1800s when thousands of schooners annually passed by on their way to and from the new Ship Canal connecting Green Bay and Lake Michigan. Though, it no longer exists as a lighthouse; the building was moved into the city of Sturgeon Bay and became a residence that is still used.

Sherwood Point Lighthouse (1883)

Location: On the northern shore of Sherwood Point about 6 miles northwest of Sturgeon Bay.

> 44 deg. 53 min. 34.0 sec. N. Latitude
> 87 deg. 26 min. 00.4 sec. W. Longitude

Viewing: There is no public access to the lighthouse grounds, but the lighthouse can be seen from a boat in summer. There is a good long-distance view of the lighthouse from Olde Stone Quarry County Park across the bay from Sherwood Point.

Summary History:
- Built May-Sept 1883 at a cost of $12,000; opened 10 Oct 1883.
- Faulty lighting equipment replaced 1892.
- Bell fog signal building constructed 1892.
- Light automated 1983, last manned US lighthouse on Great Lakes.
- Entered in National Register of Historic Places, 1983

Construction & Design: The Sherwood Point Lighthouse was constructed of red brick on a stone foundation; it included a 1½-story keeper's dwelling measuring 25 feet by 37 feet, with a light tower attached to its front. The fog signal was built of wood in 1892; it had a pyramidal shape to support the bell suspended inside.

Tower Height: 35 feet.

Height of Light Above Water: 61-foot focal plane.

Light Type: Original (1883) light unknown; in 1892, a 10-sided cast-iron lantern and a 4th-Order Fresnel lens were installed, with a 15-mile range.

Administration: US Coast Guard maintains light and leases keeper's dwelling and grounds as a private residence.

Sherwood Point Lighthouse

Sherwood Point is a narrow, fishhook-shaped peninsula six miles northwest of the city of Sturgeon Bay. It is named for Peter Sherwood who settled there around 1850, originally as a trapper and fur trader, and later a barrel maker. He was one of the first settlers in this part of Door County.

Sherwood Point Lighthouse (1883)

The lighthouse was completed in 1883. It stands on a cliff on the northern shore of Sherwood Point at the Green Bay entrance to Sturgeon Bay. It was built to aid navigation of the increasing number of ships that were passing through Sturgeon Bay after completion of the Sturgeon Bay Ship Canal.

Henry Stanley became the first keeper when he was transferred from Eagle Bluff Lighthouse. William Cochems of Sturgeon Bay became keeper in 1895. A telephone line was strung through the woods all the way to town so that the lighthouse could communicate shipping activity and problems. Cochems was responsible for keeping this phone line working.

The Sherwood Point Light holds the distinction of having been the last manned lighthouse operated by the US on the Great Lakes. It became fully automated in 1983 on its 100-year anniversary.

The keeper's residence is the only one in Door County to be constructed of red brick. The lighthouse is well maintained and very attractive with the combination of the red brick and white light tower and separate white wooden bell tower. It is now used as a private residence and there is no access to the lighthouse or grounds. The lighthouse can be clearly viewed, however, from the water and also at a distance from the county park at the old stone quarry across the bay from Sherwood Point.

On the site of the Sherwood Point Lighthouse, a pyramidal wooden structure with a pagoda-style roof stands directly in front of the lighthouse building; it housed a fog-bell signal which helped guide ships as they passed through the entrance to the outer bay of Sturgeon Bay. It was the only fog-bell signal of this type to be built at a Door County lighthouse.

The Future
of Door County Lighthouses

Fortunately, most of the lighthouses in Door County are listed on the National Register of Historic Places; being included on the National Register is very important because it reflects official public recognition of the historical value of these sites and provides some assurance that they will not be allowed to perish. The only Door County lighthouses not on the National Register are:

(1) the Old Baileys Harbor Lighthouse;

(2) the Sturgeon Bay North Pierhead Light; and

(3) the Dunlaps Reef Keeper's House [which is no longer part of a lighthouse].

The Door County Historical Society, the Door County Maritime Museum, the Ridges Sanctuary, the Coast Guard, the Wisconsin State Parks System, and many others have done a great deal to maintain and restore Door County's lighthouse sites.

Cana Island, Plum Island, and Pilot Island are owned by the federal government, but its possible that these properties may be turned over either to the State of Wisconsin or to Door County.

Seven of the existing lighthouses are still in active operation, including:

(1) Sherwood Point Lighthouse;

(2) Sturgeon Bay Ship Canal Lighthouse;

(3) Sturgeon Bay North Pierhead Light;

(4) Eagle Bluff Lighthouse;

(5) Cana Island Lighthouse;

(6) Pilot Island Lighthouse; and

(7) Plum Island Range Lights.

The technology of automation has led to the demise of lighthouse keepers in the traditional sense by making it possible to operate navigational beacons without an on-site keeper. Also, radio beacons, radar, and now GPS satellite navigation systems, all make some kinds of lighthouse operations obsolete or actually unnecessary. Three Door County lighthouses, while no longer operating, have been replaced by automated steel light towers erected on their grounds. They include:

(1) The Baileys Harbor Range Lights;
(2) Pottawatomie Lighthouse; and
(3) Chambers Island Lighthouse.

In addition, Dunlap Reef has a permanent navigational light and buoys at the site of the former lighthouse and range light.

However, the remaining active lighthouses are still very important to many vessels. They help to guide many sailors, mostly sport boaters, whose vessels lack the luxury of modern electronic navigational technology. And, for all mariners, there can be great reassurance in being able to see a light shining out of the darkness when the dark loneliness of a stormy Great Lakes night can make one doubt many things, including electronic navigational equipment and radar display screens.

Thus, many of the Door County lighthouses and range lights still have important practical uses, and all are rich in history. But they also serve now to cast another type of beacon. They light the way and remind us of an earlier, simpler, and more romantic period of tall-masted graceful schooners and the strong, determined men and women who struggled with and thrived on the waters of this peninsula of ours. Perhaps the lights of the past can help to guide us to the future.

Visitors' Guide to Door County Lighthouses & Maritime History

Door County's historic lighthouses provide visitors with an opportunity to add a new and rewarding dimension to their stay on the peninsula. Visitors will be able to see some of the area's best natural beauty, travel back to a simpler time in our history, and spend some quiet time pondering and appreciating the lifestyles and achievements of those hardy souls who battled the elements to establish a way of life in a new land.

Seeing Door County's Lighthouses

Visiting via Automobile or Bicycle. Seven of Door County's lighthouses are accessible for viewing by road, including the Dunlap Reef Keeper's House, Sturgeon Bay Ship Canal Lighthouse and North Pierhead Light, the Baileys Harbor Range Lights, Old Baileys Harbor Lighthouse, Cana Island Lighthouse, and Eagle Bluff Lighthouse.

Viewing Lighthouses from the Water. Visitors who would like to see some of Door County's lighthouses from the water, but do not have their own boat, have several options. These include passenger cruises, boat charters, boat rentals, and the Washington Island ferries. Sturgeon Bay, Fish Creek, Ephraim, and Gills Rock all have services available, and the Washington Island ferries run daily out of Northport.

Viewing Lighthouses from the Air. A truly spectacular way to see all of Door County, including the lighthouses and even some shipwrecks, is from the air. Guided air tours of various lengths and itineraries are available through the Cherryland Airport in Sturgeon Bay and through the Eagle Harbor Air Service in Ephraim.

Museums & Libraries

DOOR COUNTY LIBRARY
107 S. 4th Ave, Sturgeon Bay, 54235
Phone: (920) 743-6578

The main library has a wealth of information available on lighthouses, and the Laurie Room houses the county's most complete collection of records and books about Door County history. Access to the library's collections is also available through branch libraries located throughout the county.

DOOR COUNTY MARITIME MUSEUM — STURGEON BAY
120 N. Madison Ave, Sturgeon Bay, Wi 54235
Phone: (920) 743-5958   Web site: www.dcmm.org

The Sturgeon Bay branch of the Door County Maritime Museum is a large (20,000 square feet) new facility located at the west end of the downtown bridge that offers a spectacular overview of Door County's maritime history. The galleries include an exhibit on Door County lighthouses, an actual pilot house from a Great Lakes ore carrier, and an impressive collection of model ships, antique boats, boat motors, and marine artifacts. Sturgeon Bay's shipbuilding tradition is documented with photos, videos, and displays, and there is a gallery of maritime art with changing displays of work by different artists. The upper gallery windows provide a panorama of the bay and a fine view of shipping activity along the waterfront, including a fleet of tugboats moored at docks right in front of the museum. The museum is open all year with many special events and exhibits.

Door County Maritime Museum — Gills Rock

12724 Wisconsin Bay Rd, Gills Rock, WI 54210
Phone: (920) 854-1844   Web site: www.dcmm.org

The Maritime Museum's northern branch is located near the shore of Death's Door at the northern tip of the Door County peninsula.   The commercial fishing industry and Great Lakes shipwrecks are the facility's main focus. The *Hope*, a commercial fishing vessel, has been restored and is on display in the museum, with a dock constructed around it to allow easy visitor viewing. Exhibits of equipment, artifacts and photos chronicle Door County's fishing industry, both past and continuing.   Shipwrecks are featured in displays, including a recreated underwater exhibit with many shipwreck artifacts. Other displays include a lifesaving area with a lifeboat, a commercial ice fishing display, antique engines, a navigational display, and ship models. The facility in Gills Rock is open seasonally. Information on the Gills Rock museum is also available through the Sturgeon Bay branch of the museum.

Jackson Harbor Maritime Museum —
Washington Island

RR #1, Box 222, Washington Island, WI 54246
Phone: (920) 847-2179

The museum is located at Jackson Harbor in the far northeastern corner of Washington Island. It is housed in two former fishing sheds adjacent to docks from which commercial fishermen still operate. Artifacts, equipment, photos, and boat models give visitors an insight into the rugged and independent lifestyle of commercial fishermen. There are also displays of Coast Guard and shipwreck memorabilia. The museum offers various special interest programs during the summer season.

WISCONSIN MARITIME MUSEUM — MANITOWOC
75 Maritime Drive, Manitowoc, WI 54220
Phone: (920) 684-0218

The maritime museum in Manitowoc is not actually in Door County, but it is located only an hour's drive south of Sturgeon Bay along the Lake Michigan shore and is well worth visiting on the way to or from Door County. One of the most striking attractions at the museum is the *USS Cobia*, a US Navy submarine that was built in Manitowoc during World War II; it has been restored to its original condition and is moored adjacent to the museum, where it is open for tours. The museum also offers two floors of exhibits documenting Great Lakes shipbuilding and maritime history, including a model ship gallery that features handcrafted models of all types of Great Lakes ships from early schooners to modern ore carriers. The museum also offers special exhibits and events through the year.

Robert LaSalle County Park

An historical marker in the Robert LaSalle County Park, located near the intersection of County Roads J and U about ten miles south of Sturgeon Bay on Lake Michigan, has been erected at a site where the French explorer Robert LaSalle nearly perished as he continued his explorations southward in 1679 after parting from his famous ship, the *Griffin*. He and his men were saved by a group of friendly Potawatomi Indians.

Shipyard Tours — Sturgeon Bay

Tours of Sturgeon Bay's shipyards (sponsored by the Sturgeon Bay Rotary Club) take place in early May, offering visitors an insight into the shipbuilding industry which has been an important part of Door County's economy for many decades.

Please call the Door County Maritime Museum for information regarding these tours; please DO NOT call Palmer Johnson or Bay Shipbuilding.

Locations include:

PALMER JOHNSON INC. is a world-renowned builder of large, luxurious yachts. The vessel(s) upon which they are currently working often can be seen moored to their dock near the Michigan Avenue bridge.

BAY SHIPBUILDING CORPORATION builds and maintains many of the large cargo vessels of the Great Lakes fleet. Especially during the winter, when Great Lakes shipping is dormant, it is sometimes possible to see an array of large cargo vessels docked at Bay Shipbuilding while they are undergoing maintenance or refitting.

Door County May Lighthouse Walk

The Door County Lighthouse Walk is held in mid-May, and several mainland lighthouse locations are included. There are also boat tours to some of the island lighthouses. Advance reservations are almost always required for the popular boat tours. Selected lighthouse keeper's quarters are open for public viewing during the walk. This event is sponsored by the Door County Maritime Museum.

Washington Island Maritime Days

The Washington Island Maritime Days are held in late June at the Jackson Harbor Maritime Museum on Washington Island. The event celebrates Washington Island's long tradition of commercial fishing on Lake Michigan.

Door County Maritime Museum Classic Wooden Boat Show & Festival Days — Sturgeon Bay

The Maritime Museum's wooden and antique boat show is held in early August; it also includes model ship displays, boat building contests, Coast Guard demonstrations, and an art fair, in a two-day event. Unrelated activities include a Venetian Night boat parade, and fireworks display which also traditionally take place on the same weekend.

* * * * * * *

For more information on any of the above facilities, places, or events, call or write to the individual facilities, to local information centers, or to the Door County Chamber of Commerce.

Selected References

Frederickson, Arthur C. and Lucy F. Frederickson.
Ships and Shipwrecks in Door County Wisconsin. V1 (1961) 72 pp. & V2 (1963) 76 pp. Appleton, WI: Clark Willick. These two volumes contain photos, brief histories, and interesting stories about ships that sailed Door County waters during the past 150 years.

Hirthe, Walter M. and Mary K.
Schooner Days in Door County. (1986) 147 pp. Minneapolis, MN: Voyageur Press. This book provides a detailed account of Door County's early shipbuilding industry at Little Sturgeon Bay as well as stories and photos of several of the old ships that were built in Door County or sailed county waters.

Holand, Hjalmar R.
History of Door County, 2 volume set. (1993) 467 pp. & 484 pp. Ellison Bay, WI: Wm Caxton Ltd. This reprint of the original 1917 edition is the single best source on the early history of the county. Volume 1 consists of a narrative history of the county, arranged topically; Volume 2 contains several hundred brief biographies of early Door County residents.

Holand, Hjalmar R.
Old Peninsula Days. (1990) 252 pp. Ellison Bay, WI: Wm Caxton Ltd. This reprint of the original 1925 edition describes the people, places and events of Door County's early history. It is the author's abridgement of V1 of his *History of Door County* and is easily the most famous book ever written about Door County.

Johnson, Fred (editor)
Door County Almanak.
V1 "Premiere Issue" (1982) 144 pp.; V2 "Orchards" (1985) 224 pp.; V3 "Fishing" (1986) 336 pp.; V4 "Farms" (1987) 304 pp.; V5 "Tourism, Resorts & Transportation" (1990) 350 pp. Each of these volumes chronicles a different aspect of the history of Door County through dozens of short articles, photos and drawings.

Mielke, Phyl
>   *Eagle Bluff Journal 1895.* (1995), 127 pp. Published by the author. This charming book combines many historical facts and a fictional diary written from the point of view of the son of a lighthouse keeper to provide the reader with a sense of what early lighthouse life was like.

Murray, Robert Dickson
>   *Thunder Over The Door.* (1991), 110 pp. Ellison Bay, WI: Wm Caxton Ltd. This beautifully illustrated book presents the author's first-hand experiences of travel to Door County from 1912, when he first came to Door County at the age of six, to 1930 — when steamships provided the main means of transportation to county ports.

Olson, William H.
>   *Island Verse.* (1995) 61 pp. Washington Island, WI.: Jackson Harbor Press. This small book of poems presents Olson's reflections on life on Washington Island, lighthouse keepers, sailing ships, and commercial fishing.

Schreiber, Edward and Lois (editors)
>   *Fish Creek Voices.* (1990) 282 pp. Ellison Bay, WI.: Wm Caxton Ltd. This collection of reminiscences and oral historical accounts includes stories about Chambers Island and its lighthouse, the Duclon family of lighthouse keepers who tended the Eagle Harbor light, and the Hill Steamboat Line, along with other material concerning village residents and descendants of many of Fish Creek's founding families.